Practical Pre-School

What does it mean to be two?

A practical guide to child development

by Jennie Lindon

Contents

Introduction 2-7

A strong child 8-15

A skilful communicator 16-27

A competent learner 28-39

A healthy child 40-49

What should concern you? 50-51

Further resources 52-53

Acknowledgements 54

Published by Step Forward Publishing Limited, 25 Cross Street, Leamington Spa, Warwickshire CV32 4PX

Telephone: 01926 420046 www.practicalpreschool.com

 Illustrations by Cathy Hughes.

What does it mean to be two? ISBN: 1-904575-07-2

Introduction

Food for thought
You need to tune in to the likely perspective of two-year-olds and start where they are. What might just-twos say?

What does it mean for me to be two?

- I am independently mobile, so let me use my skills. I concentrate perfectly well on the move and outdoors.
- I like a chat, so please be patient while I get my thoughts in order.
- While I'm a young two, you probably won't understand everything I say.
- If I look puzzled, it's because your words don't make sense to me – try again more simply, or show me.
- I like getting my hands on nice play materials and I like people to join in my play - that includes you.
- Sometimes I really want to do it myself. But some of my self-care skills are a long-term, joint project.
- I want to know that you like me, whatever I have done today, and that you truly keep me in mind when we are apart.
- I like you to be my safety net, but I definitely need some adventures.
- I need to know that a cuddle is on offer whenever I want one.

What Does it Mean to be Two? **addresses the developmental needs and likely skills of two-year-olds. However, it makes sense to show how twos develop once they are three, so you will also find some examples that include older children. The way that you establish quality for under-threes is completely consistent with good practice within an appropriate early years curriculum with over-threes.**

How two-year-olds may not 'fit'

Twos are a bit of an oddity from the perspective of early years services in the UK. They can end up as two-year-old square pegs jammed into three- or four-year-old round holes. Potential problems arise from the historical split between care and education:

- Nursery schools and classes, playgroups and pre-schools catered for three- to five-year-olds and came to be labelled as early education.
- Daycare settings and childminders accepted children as young babies and were largely seen as carers.

The care-education division is total nonsense from the children's perspective. Care and learning are inseparable and good early years practice is always organised around that understanding.

Unfortunately, official statements and the structure of much inspection have persisted in presenting the two as separate. This approach would matter less if it were separate yet equal, but care and caring are so often treated as the poor relation. Undervaluing care has a negative effect on the quality of provision for three- to five-year-olds. An 'only care' outlook is even more serious for two-year-olds, because they need demonstrably more caring support.

A birth to five framework is being developed for England called the Early Years Foundation Stage. The Childcare Bill (in process at the time of writing) will make use of the framework statutory: all registered early years provision will need to work within that framework. The changes should not be overwhelming, because the main objective is to bring together *Birth to Three Matters*, the Foundation Stage curriculum for three- to five-year-olds and the National Standards applicable for different types of early years provision. The objective is also to remove the artificial care-education distinction within early years practice.

Birth to Three Matters and the *Foundation Stage Curriculum Guidance* look different. But the core values and content share a great deal of common ground. These two documents will continue to guide good practice, but the new framework will help practitioners make the connections for children's learning from the earliest months to the end of Reception class.

It is crucial that the Early Years Foundation Stage framework fully respects how children learn through the early years and the non-negotiable role of caring adults and a supportive learning environment. Problems have arisen from the rhetoric within the UK that the whole point of early years services, and early education, is to prepare young children for school. The consequence is that, without sound child development knowledge, practitioners and parents may underestimate the value of what two-year-olds are able to do, even that they are learning at all. There is a high risk of a kind of educational bullying that makes twos, and even younger children, struggle with what looks like 'proper' learning, particularly reading, writing and the more abstract mathematical activities.

When twos become your youngest children

Many pre-schools and playgroups, who previously took children no younger than three years of age, have started accepting two-year-olds to make ends meet. Such group settings now lose their older fours to Reception classes and some even lose their older threes to nursery classes. Some parents believe that only nurseries within schools can deliver early education. Sometimes, families are told that a school place cannot be guaranteed unless their children start in the nursery class.

A starting age of 2:9 (two years nine months) has often then moved to two and a half and then sometimes to two years of age. Twelve months is not long in an adult life; not much significant happens unless you have a very eventful year. However, the twelve months of developmental difference between being a 'just two' and a 'nearly three' is huge. Young twos are not simply smaller, wetter, less articulate threes: they are at a qualitatively different point in their development.

I have talked with many teams who have lowered their minimum age. I ask what changed when their group started to include two-year-olds. Some of them had already addressed potential problems and stressed the importance of positive attitudes: that the twos themselves were not being 'difficult'. On reflection, practitioners say they most noticed the following practical issues.

- Settling into a group could be much harder with the twos – both for the child and parent. Of course, separation is not simply a cheery wave goodbye for many over-threes - 'Separate from main carer with support' is one of the Stepping Stones in the English Foundation Stage for Personal, Social and Emotional Development. But the process is much tougher for many two-year-olds.
- Some settings were full of movement and sound and could be overwhelming for very young children. Making adjustments to deal with noise level and creating smaller spaces supported the less sure threes and

fours as well. Such changes often helped attention and listening.

- Young twos, even the two-and-a-halves, need more time and help with their personal care routines. These very young children are unlikely to be able to manage all their dressing, undressing and personal hygiene. They are in the process of learning self-care skills.
- Twos often want to 'do it myself' and so need time and patience. However, some children's parents are still doing practically all of their care, possibly because it's quicker. So partnership is also a key issue.
- The previous limit of three years was often explained as an age at which young children were more ready to separate from their parent(s) for a group experience. However, the advantage of passing the third birthday was that toilet training was unlikely to be an issue, apart from the odd accident. Some groups, especially pre-schools in shared premises like church halls, do not have a changing area.
- Twos need intimate personal care and this basic need has challenged some existing assumptions that 'we don't change children' or 'we don't wipe bottoms'. Serious problems can arise from unrealistic guidelines about physical contact. Quality provision cannot be maintained unless young children's toileting needs are met and that means coping with issues arising from close physical contact (see also page 11).
- The average two-year-old is smaller than threes and fours. This difference is sometimes enough that the youngest children cannot manage some furniture or bathroom fittings. The practical problem was often solved through getting a safe set of little steps.
- Small twos may have to stretch up and over some styles of water or sand trolleys. If the equipment cannot be lowered, the practical answer is to offer natural materials in smaller containers, such as bowls or trays.
- Twos are at a noticeably different stage with their communication skills. Reflective practitioners have described that they needed to adjust the way they talked with these younger children. Adults needed to allow more tuning-in time to understand two-year-olds' expressive skills.
- All the twos, especially the young ones, needed much more emotional support and special objects to be respected like their cuddlies, blanket or a dummy.
- Even with support, twos could not be expected to manage the kind of turn taking that was within the abilities of the threes and fours. As a whole, teams said they had to re-adjust their expectations for a wide range of everyday behaviour.
- Twos were often not able, or did not want, to join whole group story or circle time. This often led child-focused teams to reconsider the timing of any whole group activity and the size of the group. The reluctance of some twos highlighted how some older children struggled with large group activities. Rethinking the organisation of the session, or size of the group, often helped threes and fours as well.

I have observed that two-year-olds especially struggle in settings where practice has tipped too much towards adult-initiated and structured activities, especially of a neat table-top nature. The threes and fours may put up some resistance to being moved around activities 'to ensure that everyone experiences the whole curriculum'. They may become creative in their attempts to avoid misguided conveyer-belt art of the 'everybody has to paint their cut-out lighthouse' variety. But the twos can wail and throw a serious wobbler.

Wise teams had rethought their planning and whether it needed to be more flexible for all the children. Twos enjoy many of the play resources that would be available for the threes and fours. They need a bit more careful watching with some tools, but if adults are close by then most materials will not pose problems if offered in a flexible way, and that approach is good practice with over-threes too.

When twos are in a day nursery or centre

Full daycare settings deal with the practical issues of personal care. However, play and learning issues can still arise for two-year-olds who attend a full day childcare setting.

It is an advantage for all the children when different age groups spend some time together. However, that time can highlight that the twos often approach play resources in a different way from the threes and fours. Some years ago I was making observations in a day nursery where they had recently re-organised the rooms. The result was that two-year-olds had time with practitioners without the threes and fours. The team had already reflected on how they needed to adjust the adult-planned activities, especially table-top art and craft. Their own observations had made them realise, with hindsight, that the twos had hovered on the outside of such activities, while the approach had been more geared to three- and four-year-old skills.

Two-year-olds who attend a full age range early years setting usually face the move from the twos' or toddlers' room into another, often called the pre-school room. This transition should be smooth in terms of care and learning because the children know the setting. They need to get used to less familiar practitioners and the new room. Wise, child-centred teams take time and care over this transition, because some young children will be sad to leave the room and staff they know well. Good practice in the next room should provide a seamless move in terms of an accessible learning environment. There may be different kinds of challenge for learning, but still of a friendly kind.

Unwise teams say bluntly that it is big change for children to join the pre-school room, as if the statement is not open to challenge. Unfortunately, those staff often

Food for thought

The Birth to Three materials to support good practice with under-threes are very welcome for England and Scotland. But it is symbolic that they have been the last to emerge after details on the school curriculum for each country in the UK, followed by early years curriculum frameworks for threes to fives (fours in Northern Ireland).

A logical, developmentally wise approach would have been to establish the details of good practice with our very youngest children and then move up the age range. It is hard not to see the reverse chronological order as a reflection of how the very youngest children are undervalued.

This approach has also meant that early years practitioners are left with an under-threes and over-threes division. A more sensible approach would have been to develop a coherent early years framework up to formal school. Such frameworks, like the New Zealand *Te Whariki,* then show appropriate variation for babies, toddlers and children within the detail. In Scotland, South Lanarkshire created a birth to five framework in 1999.

In England the Early Years Foundation Stage, being developed as a birth to five framework, aims to bring the different guidance together as a coherent whole.

Food for thought

The structure of *Birth to Three Matters* for England has made the materials vulnerable to misguided teams or advisers trying to use it like an under-threes curriculum. There has also been a struggle to find a paperwork format that will transfer to the Foundation Stage.

All the materials were produced to fit an envelope box, rather than being an A4 file like the Foundation Stage materials. I persevered for a full year and then used a second pack to create a ring binder.

I printed the component cards off the CD Rom and then it was possible to see both sides of the card at the same time – no more flipping to and fro. I used a highlighter pen to mark up some key points. I have personalised my file with support material printed off the CD Rom and features from magazines.

The file option means that useful materials get out of the box and this option has been welcomed whenever I come across practitioners who have not already taken this approach. Where twos are the youngest in a group setting, teams can easily highlight material that is directly relevant to these young children, rather than babies and toddlers.

harass colleagues responsible for the twos' room to 'get the children ready' for unrealistic demands of 'early education'. In such settings the over-structured, adult-led activities in the pre-school room are not consistent with the Foundation Stage curriculum document.

Birth to Three: suitable frameworks for very early learning

You will be familiar with the early years guidance for over-threes. It is important to give time to read these booklets and files – for England, Scotland, Wales and Northern Ireland. Each early years curriculum guidance supports a rich, play-based curriculum, use of routines to support learning and a flexible learning environment. Each document is, in the main, well grounded in realistic expectations for the age group. Unwise practice tends to be grounded in anxiety about 'getting children ready for school' and ignoring the detailed guidance.

However, none of the curriculum documents were designed to be used with two-year-olds; they are specifically aimed at children from three to five or six years (four in Northern Ireland). From 2004 Wales has been introducing a coherent Foundation Phase to provide continuity for children from three through to seven years of age within a play-based curriculum, that will run into the early years of primary school.

England and Scotland have directly addressed quality for the under-threes. In England there is a *Birth to Three Matters* framework. In Scotland, *Birth to Three: Supporting our Youngest Children* was launched in January 2005 with a guide for parents. Further support materials have followed.

The English and Scottish birth to three materials have a different appearance and overall structure, but otherwise they have much in common, because the teams drew on the same source materials.

- *Birth to Three Matters* was informed by a substantial review from a team led by Tricia David. The development of *Birth to Three* was supported by a comprehensive report from the team led by Colwyn Trevarthen.
- Both frameworks place a strong emphasis on the importance of attachment and of close, affectionate relationships for young children. They clearly state that good quality in group care is not possible without a proper key person system.
- Both the English and Scottish teams decided not to call their birth to three guidance an under-threes curriculum. Previously, some good local guidelines had appeared in England and Scotland using the word 'curriculum'. It was a risky choice because the word carries the message that early learning should link with school skills.
- Each framework promotes the importance of a home-like atmosphere and says that good practice with very young children is influenced by what can work well in family life. The consistent message is that under-threes are young children; they are not little pupils. Their environment needs to be a home-like nursery or home not a classroom.
- Nurseries are not family homes, but the best group settings have a relaxed, home-like atmosphere - for all the children and not only the youngest. Childminders have a head start when it comes to opportunities for personal relationships and a family atmosphere.
- The birth to three frameworks, and any local under-threes guidance, all

> make it clear that childminders should be encouraged to operate in this way. There must be no sense that a drive for quality requires them to turn their homes into mini-nurseries.

The Ofsted framework for inspection in England is now strongly focused on the question, 'What is it like for a child here?' Early years practitioners are responsible for showing how they use the good practice described in guidance within their work: child-focused, play-rich practice for two-year-olds, as well as for other young children. The English *Birth to Three Matters* looks different from the Scottish *Birth to Three* guidance, but there is much of value in both documents for all practitioners. The English pack is stronger on specific ideas of what to do and how to be alert to early developments. The Scottish approach is clearer on the foundations: how practice needs to be built around relationships, responsive care and respect.

How to be a helpful adult to the twos

It is complicated to explain and predict how young children manage some of their impressive developmental achievements. For instance, no single theory can fully explain how toddlers learn to speak one, and often more than one, language within the very early years. But the consistent messages about how we can help do not point to complex techniques. The best interactions, experiences and opportunities for twos are straightforward. What benefits young learning is simple, for instance see the section about communication on page 21. But practitioners - and parents - do not always behave in these ways.

Some difficulties arise because uncertain practitioners believe they should be acting more like their memory of a primary school teacher. (An issue discussed in *What Does it Mean to be Three?*, pages 7-9.) Some practitioners may also dismiss the simpler ideas as 'just common sense'. But as the Scottish *Birth to Three* points out (page 8), 'What may seem like common sense to one person may not appear so to another and it is important that intuition - the feeling that something is right - is informed intuition. Informed intuition is based upon both knowledge and experience'.

A strong child

Food for thought

The first three principles within the Introduction booklet for the English *Birth to Three Matters* state clearly that good practice has to be built on close relationships:

- Parents and families are central to the well-being of the child.
- Relationships with other people (both adults and children) are of crucial importance in a child's life.
- A relationship with a key person at home and in the setting is essential to young children's well-being.

The Scottish *Birth to Three* is built around the 'three Rs' for effective practice: relationships, responsive care and respect.

The research review gave the clear practical message that very young children need consistent and affectionate company. The practical conclusion drawn was that good quality care depends upon creating stable and intimate relationships with practitioners who take time to get to know children and their parents as individuals.

The guidance states, 'Key to making the most of young children's capabilities is the quality of the warm, affectionate and responsive relationships surrounding babies and young children. Children become confident, independent and most resilient where they are secure in the relationships around them'. (page 11)

The importance of relationships

Attachment is key to emotional health and young children's strongest and enduring attachments should be within their family. However, two-year-olds whose parents have job or study obligations can be with childminders or nurseries for many of their waking hours during the week. It is crucial – a non-negotiable part of quality in the service – that these very young children are able to make a close relationship of affection and shared experiences with their childminder, their key person in a group setting, and steadily with other familiar practitioners in a team. Such emotional closeness can raise dilemmas about the professional balance between commitment and detachment.

Early years practitioners are often concerned that young children will become too attached to them. Maybe parents' words or facial expression communicate that they feel uneasy that 'my child likes you so much'. This adult problem needs to be faced because children's needs come first. Two-year-olds will feel emotionally insecure if you distance yourself from individual children. Young boys and girls, not just the twos, will take this as a personal rejection.

Fortunately young children do not have a small store of affection that is then emptied. Parents' reservations need to be discussed not 'solved' by making it hard for young children to form attachments in out-of-home care. It is tough, but parents need to recognise that shared care means shared affection. Parents also have to use their home time to build shared experiences that ground strong family bonds.

The *Birth to Three Matters* materials focus on relationships within the aspects of 'A healthy child' as well as 'A strong child' – one of many reminders that children's development does not fit into separate boxes. On the component card for 'Emotional well-being' in 'A healthy child' the 'Development matters' section highlights that, 'Young babies are social beings. They crave close attachments with a special person within their setting. Warm, mutual, affirmative relationships give babies the courage to express their feelings. When young children have a close relationship with a caring and responsive adult, they explore from a safe place to which they can return.'

The key person system

Individual childminders are the key person for children in their care. Day nurseries and other group settings have to establish a proper key person system to ensure the emotional safety of young children. Peter Elfer's research (explained in *Key Persons in the Nursery*, see Resources page 52) has highlighted the variety in practice of what different nurseries call their key person system. It can be a named person who:

- Takes responsibility for paperwork, completing written records, liaising and making sure that everyone in the setting is aware of the background information on the child and family. In some group settings this administrative and informational role is all that 'key person' means.
- Forms a special relationship with individual children to help them settle in. In this interpretation of key person, children are then encouraged to relate to all the other staff in a room, or the whole setting when a pre-school operates in one large space.
- Is known to parents as the person for them to contact about their child or other nursery issues.
- Establishes a special ongoing relationship with a child and family, not only for a settling-in period but for the longer-term, perhaps the child's entire time at the setting.

The last variation is the most resisted. Some practitioners, including some managers, are uneasy about the prospect of a continuing emotional closeness and see it as incompatible with a professional outlook. However, true early years professionalism blends commitment to young children and their families with a careful sense of detachment that allows practitioners to set a boundary to their working day.

Peter Elfer, and other researchers in this field, have highlighted that the difference between good and emotionally less safe nurseries can be observed in terms of personal relationships with children:

- How well do practitioners know the children for whom they are responsible? Caring adults need to become familiar with two-year-olds as individuals – and of course with younger and slightly older children, too.
- Do practitioners feel that it is acceptable to allow children to get close to them – sometimes literally in their arms? Individual or whole team reservations about emotional and physical closeness will be communicated to twos through body language. Young children can only make sense of a lack of welcome as 'you don't like me' – very serious when twos spend many of their waking hours in out-of-home care.
- Is there support from colleagues for a key person who is settling a child or whose key child is distressed? It is normal within development that twos will cry and cling when they are uncertain, unhappy or unwell.
- When teams and managers are secure in their child development knowledge, the key person will be able to relax and address the child's needs. Young children will be at risk if practitioners are made to feel they lack professional skills, because they cannot stop a child crying.
- Is there easy support for staff to talk about their own feelings for children or how to maintain a caring and professional approach? It can never be professional for practitioners to be unmoved by a child's distress, nor to withhold physical and emotional comfort.

Food for thought

The developmental needs of under-threes, that are highlighted so strongly in the English *Birth to Three Matters* and Scottish *Birth to Three*, apply wherever non-family practitioners take care of young children. There is no get-out clause for group care.

Knowledgeable nursery teams, who have established good practice, do not try to challenge the importance of close, affectionate relationships for young children. Unfortunately, some teams try to justify emotional distance with statements like, 'Group care is different'. Or they offer the justification that parents choose a nursery, in preference to a nanny or a childminder, because they do not want their children to get close to non-family adults.

Neither of these excuses stands up against a safe perspective based on child development knowledge. The needs of young children apply no matter where, or with whom, they spend their days.

In no way must two-year-olds – or threes and fours for that matter - be pushed to fit a group care convenience model. Good practice on partnership can never be to excuse bad practice with 'But that's what parents want!' (See also the Food for Thought box on page 38.)

Of course, the practitioner is not the child's parent and it would be unprofessional to criticise parents. However, even experienced staff can benefit from non-judgemental support to talk through practical issues around sharing the care of young children. If a manager truly judges that a practitioner has lost a sense of boundaries, then that dilemma needs to be addressed through the supervision system. It is irresponsible for a manager to solve their concerns by suddenly moving a practitioner to a room away from their key child, who is clearly attached, because they judge the adult and child to be too close.

Continuity of care between the family home and out-of-home care is crucial for young children's sense of well-being. So partnership with the parents of two-year-olds still needs easy and detailed communication over personal care routines. This open communication is best undertaken between the key person and parent(s) or other family carer(s). Young children grow in confidence when they can steadily share in their own care (more on page 43). Ideally the key person undertakes the personal care of their key children.

- At the very least, the key person takes responsibility through the settling process and so is able to become familiar with a child's preferred routines for changing or toileting, mealtimes and sleep or rest times.
- What can this two-year-old manage and how? Do they have personal words to express their toileting needs?
- What do they need in terms of routine or comfort to ease their transition into sleep or rest time?
- What is this two-year-old likely to find familiar or unfamiliar about meal or snack times in this setting compared with family life?

For example

Good visual examples of how a key person should work include:

- Section one, 'Trusting relationships', of the *Key Times* video (see Resources, page 53). This features comments from parents and footage of a practitioner supporting a young child through his first day. She stays close to this young boy, helps him begin to become familiar with the play resources and routines, but with no sense of pressure. She is his safe place and he can choose when and how far to move away.
- In section two, 'Physical and emotional dependence', another practitioner is responsive to his key child who is having a tough day. The little girl is upset, initially for no apparent reason, although it emerges soon that she is not very well. But her key person is there to reassure and comfort her, with words and the cuddling that she clearly wants.
- In the section 'Feeling and communicating' in the video *Tuning in to Children* (see Resources, page 53), you can observe Marcus, who is the key person for several children in the setting. The sequence shows how he greets children as they come in that morning. His words and body language communicate that he is really pleased to see each child and interested to hear what they have to say. He is ready with a cuddle for those children who want to greet him in that way. He has made the choice to be sitting down so his eye contact is level with theirs. This means that when he talks with a parent, he looks upwards.

Twos need to feel they belong

Part of being treated as an individual is that two-year-olds feel they have a place in their out-of-home care – sessional as well as full day care. Even in a regular drop-in twos are pleased to realise that they are familiar to the practitioner who runs the sessions. So it is important that you make time for hellos and goodbyes. Offer a personal welcome to young children and help to manage the transition when twos are moving from their parent(s)' full responsibility into yours and then back again at the end of a day or session.

For example

I enjoyed going with Ben (two years six months) and his mother to a regular session where a small group of twos enjoyed a music and story time. The leader of this session had taken the trouble to learn all the children's names and was able to greet children personally, even when they had not been for a few weeks. He then held the attention of these very young children because he was enthusiastic, continued to engage all the children individually and gave them the choice of whether to join in or just watch.

The Scottish *Birth to Three* guidance highlights that adult sensitivity helps young children to feel reassured of their own importance to you. Sensitivity is shown through behaviour that lets children know they are being 'kept in mind - so that even in the busiest times of the day, young children feel secure that they have not been forgotten, by being given a smile, by being talked to, by being noticed (page 17).

Touch and physical contact

In friendly communication two-year-olds like to be close. When they feel at ease with their important adults, twos move right in, tucking themselves into your arm or draping themselves over a shoulder. Your accessibility creates stronger two-year-olds, who feel confident that they are welcome, liked and emotionally safe in their out-of-home care.

- Two-year-olds need to feel reassured that a cuddle and other forms of touch are available if they are distressed, unwell or just a bit uncertain. Undoubtedly, it can be wearing for adults when a two-year-old is emotionally needy in this way. But young children become more able to cope through knowing that you will hold them and contain their distress. You neither try to avoid them nor jolly them out of legitimate feelings.
- But twos also need the physical welcome of touch and a cuddle that says you are a safe place, from which a young child can venture when they are ready to explore the indoor or outdoor resources of your setting. Friendly and respectful touch communicates, 'I'm paying attention to you' or 'That is so interesting! I'm just as excited about the huge worm as you are'.

The lovely phrase 'snuggling in' is used several times in *Birth to Three Matters*. The wording means two equally important parts of good practice.

- Snuggling in means giving a warm and responsive attachment to individual children through physical contact. The component card for 'A sense of belonging' focuses on the importance for young children of 'acquiring social confidence and competence including being able to snuggle in, enjoy being with familiar and trusted others'. The message is that children need to be able to snuggle onto a lap or just rest their head against someone, stroking a cheek or holding a hand.
- But snuggling in also means that a young child's environment offers small and cosy spaces - child-sized places of peacefulness. In the same component card part of effective practice is to 'Recognise that young babies will find comfort from "snuggling in" with a variety of objects and people in different places, such as cosy corners with soft inviting surfaces.'

Food for thought

Community Playthings, the nursery equipment manufacturers, consult with a range of early years professionals when they are in the process of developing a new item.

They asked me to comment on the nursery 'Welcome area' that was at the development stage. They wanted a flexible furniture system that met practical needs like storage for outdoor shoes or coats. But an equally important aim was to communicate a clear 'Pleased to see you!' message to children and parents.

I realised as we discussed possibilities that the welcome area is also the goodbye area. It is a chance to communicate to children especially that 'this is your nursery', 'you have your own special place in this pre-school' and 'we will keep you in mind until we meet again'.

In what ways can you personalise your welcome area to show to children who leave for the day, 'We'll be thinking of you – see you soon!'?

Being a helpful adult

Supportive early years practitioners let young children know that they are definitely not out of sight - out of mind. You let two-year-olds know that they are 'kept in mind' because within the day or session:

- You make comments like, 'Clyde, I haven't seen you for a little while. Have you been busy digging in the garden?'
- You start a simple conversation that lets two-year-olds know that you remember what they enjoyed yesterday. Perhaps you have cleared more space so Simone and her friend can recreate their spaceship.
- You have not forgotten that Ria told you on Friday that her family was going to visit Grandma at the weekend. So, during Monday's session, you ask about the visit.
- You can use conversation, photos and little treasure boxes of home items to reassure young children that they are kept in mind by their families during their day with you.

The strong message from both the English and Scottish birth to three research reviews is that adults have to be generous with physical contact. Otherwise, secure and trusting relationships cannot be built with young children. If uncertain early years practitioners need to ask 'Can we cuddle?' the developmentally correct answer for the children is 'definitely yes!' So how have some nursery teams become uncertain to the point of stepping back from touch, even from children as young as two years of age?

The usual justification from a team is to point to child protection. But the specific fear is about allegations of sexual abuse and is a misrepresentation of good practice over child protection. Physically and emotionally distant practitioners could be legitimately challenged that their behaviour was potentially neglectful or bordered on emotional abuse. In England, a particular sentence in the *Guidance to the National Standards* seems to have caused much of the anxiety along the lines of 'you have to watch your back!' In Standard 13 on Child Protection the full day care booklet has the statement 'It is important that staff avoid putting themselves in situations that may lead to allegations being made against them' (page 55)

This sentence appears to be the source of nursery decisions that there must always be two adults present when a child is receiving intimate personal care and some of the no-cuddling guidelines. I have heard reliable accounts that some Ofsted inspectors do favour such rules. But equally, others have looked for other indications that a team understands child protection for very young children. The sentence does not appear in the equivalent childminding guidance.

It is impossible to envisage how practitioners in group settings could withhold physical contact and yet still meet the requirements from another section of the English National Standards. In Standard 3, 'Care, Learning and Play' (page 15) for full day care the guidance stresses the importance of 'Building positive relationships and developing self-esteem. You can help children develop their confidence and independence by providing a warm and secure environment where staff:

- are friendly and approachable
- are positive and respectful of children of all backgrounds and abilities
- give reassurance, encouragement and appropriate praise
- value each child and what they have to offer.'

For example

The visual images in the *Birth to Three Matters* video are all supportive of close physical contact and comfortable touch between practitioners and young children. For instance:

- See how close the practitioner is to all the children as they sing a song (early during the video). One child sits on her lap.
- Another visual message is given by the sequence where a childminder enjoys a book with a young child and a baby. All of them are close and relaxed.
- In the later personal care sequence, the practitioner looks fully comfortable with touching a young child as she changes his nappy and she remains very close as they move together through a handwashing routine.

The *Birth to Three Matters* video provides a clear visual message of what really counts as good practice with very young children. The *Key Times* video (see Resources, page 53) also offers examples of young children sitting close, on an adult's lap, leaning against a back or shoulder. There are similar examples of good and respectful touch in *The High/Scope Approach for Under-Threes* (see Resources, page 53). Young children show every confidence that an adult's arms and lap are available – as a comfortable seat and a play space just as much as for when they are upset.

A balance between me and other people

Two-year-olds are very much individuals and in a home situation that individuality can flourish. Group provision needs to be carefully balanced so that two-year-olds can gain an emotionally healthy sense of belonging, that 'This is my room' or 'This is my pre-school' without any doubts that they are noticed. Two-year-olds are egocentric in a positive sense; they are at the centre of their social world. Twos who feel confident that they are liked and cherished as an individual show that they have the intellectual and emotional capacity to begin to put themselves into someone else's shoes.

For example

These two descriptions, from the *Key Times* folder (see Resources, page 53), show how much two-year-olds can 'step back' mentally, so long as their thoughts are based on something familiar. Faith is able to comment about herself, and Billie, to imagine being like her friend. Both examples come from the section about 'Their growing sense of themselves as individuals'.

Two-year-old Faith was playing with other twos, making marks with finger paint. Using her hand, Faith spread a mid-brown colour up her arm and said 'Look, it me'. The practitioner, thinking Faith had said, 'Look at me', replied with, 'I can see you, you're spreading the paint on your arm.' Faith came back with, 'No, it me, me' and the practitioner now understood the message and said, 'Oh yes! It is like you, it is the colour of your skin, a lovely brown.' The children started to copy Faith's action and the practitioner fetched a mirror so they could all see the effects of the paint on their skin, seeing whose skin matched the brown paint. After lunch the practitioner added other skin tones to the available paints and also added a bowl of water so that the children could easily see the paint washed away but their skin remained the same tone (page 7). This is a good example of how early years practitioners can build on children's interests when they are close and attentive to play.

Billie and Meg (both girls aged two and a half) had developed a close friendship. Meg was unable to speak as a result of her cerebral palsy, but the two children communicated in play and clearly enjoyed each other's company. Billie's mother reported that her daughter liked to play at 'being Meg' at home. During this play Billie had to be carried or used a piece of cardboard as a standing frame. Billie's mother and her key person agreed that Billie was exploring and imagining what it was like to be her friend. Billie's play was in no way demeaning of Meg's condition, nor was Billie regressing in her own development (page 3). This example also shows well the importance of partnership: that Billie's mother was able to talk with the key person, sharing these details of play at home, and possibly be reassured.

Two-year-olds can be definite about what they think and want – sometimes right this minute! But, again with adult support, they become more able to express personal opinions and preferences, modified somewhat from a blunt 'I want' or 'No, not that!' Creative approaches to consulting with young children have stretched sometimes down to twos as well as very young threes. You will find discussion of some of these projects in *What Does it Mean to be Three?* (page 14) and *What Does it Mean to be Four?* (page 23).

Two-year-olds can express their views and preferences. Young twos need simple approaches geared to today, indeed right now. But older twos and rising threes become more able, with experience, to express preferences and contribute to decisions. It is easy when you use what Mark Gladwin and others (*Consulting Children about Play* - see Resources, page 52) call the 'golden methods':

- You watch what children choose to do within their play using the resources of your home as a childminder or a group setting. Their behaviour will tell you what is important, what are the special places and most favoured equipment or other resources.
- Encourage young children to talk with you. They will learn to express their views when you show respect by paying attention to what they say and show that you would genuinely like to understand their perspective.

These basic and workable methods let the twos know and believe that you are genuinely interested in what they think and that their views can make a difference. This experience supports them as they pass through this year and other methods of simple consultation become possible.

Older twos and young threes are able to express views, often supported by something visual – that either they or you provide. Try these methods, adjusted for the age and understanding of the very young children. The visual element continues to be helpful with over-threes who are fluent in a language that you do not speak and children whose disabilities make communication less easy.

- Older twos and young threes may well do you a drawing out of choice and tell you what is in the drawing. Young children may use their painting to say that Little Monster is sad because he never gets to play with the train.
- Young children may comment spontaneously about a story or a picture in a story, that lets you know what is on their mind, for example that 'We never go to the park any more!' Sensible adults realise that 'never' often means 'We haven't been to the park for ages' and do not argue about 'never'.
- Some older twos are ready to use the visual opportunities of a camera – either for them to operate or to direct you to take pictures of what is 'important' indoors or outside. Alison Clark and Peter Moss (*Spaces to*

Play: More Listening to Young Children - see Resources, page 52) established this word as an alternative to 'favourite' or 'special'. It is a useful word because a resource may be important in some way without being a favourite.

- Young children give adults a tour, either after the photos are developed or sometimes as part of directing you to take a photo. Children's comments let you know, for instance, that a playhouse or other outdoor den is important to them. However, the current structure is too small – look at how me and my friends are all squashed up! Buying a bigger playhouse may not be a viable option. However, you and the children may be able to find ways to extend the resource, perhaps creating temporary structures using large cardboard boxes.
- Twos can understand the symbolism of a picture or photo, so appropriate illustrations can help them to choose between options, for example of food for a picnic. In a relaxed atmosphere two-year-olds may choose to tell you why they would prefer Marmite sandwiches to cheese. The same approach can work well to encourage twos to be part of choosing flowers or vegetables for the garden.
- Visual support can be three-dimensional as well as flat images. Two-year-olds can start to plan their own activities from what is on offer. They may use words alone or you could lay out a tray with an example of items from different parts of an accessible learning environment. You can see this method used with a large tray in the video *The High/Scope Approach with Under-Threes* (see Resources, page 53).

It is crucial that any consultation is genuine. Even twos and rising threes will get irritated if they are asked to express preferences yet their important adults appear to take no notice of what has been said. Young children also get annoyed when they realise that an adult is trying to talk them round to an adult decision that has already been made.

A skilful communicator

Twos are using their voice

The fifth principle offered in the Introduction booklet for *Birth to Three Matters* is that 'Learning is a shared process and children learn most effectively when, with the support of a knowledgeable and trusted adult, they are actively involved and interested'. This approach is sensible with twos, whatever you are doing, but especially useful if you want to encourage twos to be skilful communicators. Young children need plenty of relaxed opportunities to talk as well as listen. Their language skills, as well as general learning, will be stunted if adults see communication mainly as 'I talk – you listen' or 'My questions are more important than yours'.

If all is going well, two-year-olds have the power of language on their side. They are busy making meaning of their world and their voices can now be as busy as their hands and feet. But they are also learning about the purpose and uses of their language. Their experiences in out-of-home care can shape their understanding, just as much as their family experiences – 'Do adults think that what I have to say is interesting?' 'Is my being nice and quiet more important to them than hearing me express my thoughts?'

Listen for different kinds of words

For young two-year-olds the whole question of vocabulary should have moved beyond simply counting how many words they use. It is important to recall how expressive language starts.

- Toddlers' first words are those that name familiar people and objects, such as 'Mama', 'dog' or 'juice', although they usually pronounce many of these less than accurately. They then work out that you use the same word for a picture of a banana or a cat as you do for the real thing. Grammatically speaking, these words are nouns.
- Once toddlers have a fair number of naming words, they start to use words for actions like 'jump'. They also combine two words in a way that communicates doing something, for instance, 'getup' to indicate 'I want to get up – please lift me' or 'I have climbed up – look at me!'. They also use words that describe that something has happened, like 'gone' or 'broken'. In terms of grammar, these words are verbs and parts of verbs.
- Fortunately, toddlers and young twos do not try to speak in a grammatically correct way. They work happily with what they have and use what Annette Karmiloff-Smith calls 'pivot words' (*Baby it's You* - see Resources, page 52). These are words or word-like, flexible terms that are hard to classify grammatically. At two

years old, Tanith used a number of these pivot words (see the example on page 18). Annette Karmiloff-Smith (page 157, *Baby it's You*) describes Rowan at 20 months who added 'me' to create a useful way of asking or commanding – 'shoe me!' 'apple me!' Jimmy at 23 months used 'nogoin' that worked well as a general negative, for instance, 'nogoin juice' and 'nogoin nightnight' (to bed).

- Older toddlers start to combine naming and action words in ways that make sense to them and which meet a range of communication needs. Their very short phrases leave out any linking words but still make sense to familiar adults who listen, watch and take the clues from context and body language. From the *Baby it's You* project (pages 157 and 161), Joshua at 19 months expressed 'naughty car broken' and Stacey at 20 months described 'doggy gone'. Gillian at 23 months was able to construct, 'Mummy ring broken', 'Gilly knee hurt', 'Gilly got car' and a firm 'No in bath'.

Older toddlers, who have a range of naming and action words, then start to say words that describe people or things (adjectives) or actions (adverbs). It is important that practitioners polish up this part of child development knowledge. Otherwise they try to get young children to tackle abstract concepts before they are able to understand and use these words.

- Descriptive words make no sense for young children until they can hook them to a noun or verb. For instance, 'dark' does not exist alone. The night or late afternoon winter sky is dark, a room may be dark until the light is switched on. A word like 'fast' means nothing unless it is linked to an action, such as running fast or the toy car that a child pushes fast along the floor. These words refer to abstract concepts and young children grasp them a bit at a time, within a tangible context for sense (see also page 31).
- Older twos start to get the idea that some naming words include a whole group of people or things, such as animals or fruit. These category nouns are difficult and twos often struggle for a while – all daddies are men but not all men are daddies. Two-year-old mistakes are logical and related to discovering the boundaries to the use of a word. As a young two, Drew was confused for a while about foxes and classified them as cats – an understandable mistake. By two years four months, he had realised they were different animals. He enjoyed pointing to a picture and announcing, 'Fox, like a cat'.
- Twos will have grasped that people and objects have names: a significant intellectual shift. Children then ask by words or a questioning tone to communicate, 'What's that?'. They expand their own vocabulary by actively learning the words for what they want to say.
- So, within their year of being two, young children develop a significant vocabulary – enough that it becomes a tough task to write it all down. They start to understand and use other kinds of words and they are able to link their existing vocabulary into short sentences. They use simple words for position, like 'in', 'off', 'under' or 'behind'.
- You will hear some twos use mainly correct words to indicate a time

Food for thought

Very young toddlers may have a few words that defy being categorised by grammar. These words/phrases are from what they have heard other people say. When you know a very young child and listen, then you will realise that they are acute imitators. They will sometimes produce phrases that you recognise as your own, even down to your intonation, such as 'Ohdearyme'. Toddlers use these words/phrases in a correct context.

- Ben, at just a year, started to say 'Wowlookadat!' to direct people's attention to anything of interest. He had heard this phrase from his mother and older cousins on a family holiday. The children had taken delight in walking Ben around to show him the natural world. As young as he was, Ben imitated this phrase and then used it accurately to get people to look at what he found interesting.
- Drew at close to two years used his grandfather's jokey phrase of 'Justaminute!' to indicate that he would be available very soon. Drew sometimes said the phrase as 'Justaminute-Gramps!', showing his recognition that this was the special phrase of one person in the family.

sequence: 'now', 'later', 'when', 'after'. Drew, at two years three months, said, 'Baby milk when finished hold her' – a phrase that does not make much sense until you know that he was sitting beside me, while I fed his baby sister. Drew knew Tanith needed to finish her feed. But he was letting me know that, after that, he wanted her placed on his lap for a little while.

- Young children need to hear different words in context, said clearly by adults or older children. Twos will then start to use those words themselves and be able to practise. Soon you will hear the words that link together different thoughts or a line of two-year-old reasoning: words like 'if', 'but', 'because', 'so'.
- The older twos and young threes have a more theoretical understanding of spoken language and can be sticklers for accuracy. For example, Janet at two years 11 months (in the *Baby it's You* project - see Resources, page 52) is described by her mother: 'Janet has started asking questions about language. Like she'll ask what something is called and then she'll ask why it's called that.' By three years one month: 'Janet corrects her baby brother now – if he says "bockle", she shouts, "No boTTle!"' The emphasis (in original) shows how Janet sounded that part of the word that she had identified her brother said wrongly.

For example

By the time she had reached her second birthday, it was hard to keep track of Tanith's expressive language – the vocabulary she used herself in her speech. We had noted by then more than 150 single words but she was already combining them into many two-word phrases and a few simple phrases with three words, such as 'Daddy do it' and 'Let me look'.

Tanith used a mixture of naming, action and descriptive words. She showed understanding (receptive language) in a familiar context of more words than she actually said – the usual situation for a just two.

- Her vocabulary included the names of all the familiar people in her life, most of the food and drink she liked, the names for animals she could see in the neighbourhood and those featured in her favourite books. She combined a naming word with 'on' or 'off' – usually to make a request, for example, 'beads on', 'clothes off'.
- She used single words to describe her own, or other people's actions, by saying 'swimming', 'digging', 'splashing' and 'eating'. I observed that Tanith probably used the '-ing' format in imitation of my usual way of commenting to her, for instance, 'You're kicking the ball'.
- Tanith also used action words with other simple words, usually to voice a request for somebody else to do something, for instance, 'shut it' and 'hold it'. It took me a short while to work out that her phrase 'help it' was a request for help, but 'help me' was an offer to help. I understood why Tanith had created these combinations when I listened to myself. I regularly said, 'Do you want some help with it?' when she was struggling with her clothes. But when she came into the kitchen my usual phrase was, 'Do you want to help me?'. Tanith also said 'come too', either to indicate that she wanted to accompany someone or to ask somebody in the family to come and join her where she wished to be.
- Tanith spontaneously used a range of descriptive words. She used 'hot', 'warm' and 'cold', also with the further description of 'nose bit cold' and 'very warm'. She had 'tasty' and 'crunchy' (for food), 'light' and 'dark', four colour words that she used accurately herself, 'gentle', 'sticky' (for her hands or the gluey state of her picture), 'squeaky', 'noisy' and 'big bang', 'long' and 'big'.
- Within two months Tanith was forming sentences (see the examples on page 20). She also understood enough about language to make verbal jokes that depended on saying something she knew to be incorrect. Tanith thought that 'hot sandwich' was a real winner, because the idea was so ridiculous (we did not own a toasted sandwich maker). She liked telling people that they were somebody else, for instance 'you baby Anna', followed by chortles and 'just teasing' or 'just pretend'.

Two-year-olds are able to recall past experiences and ask questions that show they remember.

For example:

- Ben at two years six months asked questions with confidence – 'What is happening?' 'Where are we going?' 'What's under there?' But he also clearly recalled and talked about events in the recent past.
- He reminded his mother how they came to visit (nearly two weeks earlier) and Ben played with water and containers at my kitchen sink.
- Ben returned to playgroup in the new year after a break of a month and asked straightaway 'Where's Mr Ben?' (the male playgroup worker).

If you do not know children well yet, you may lack key items of information to make sense of their narrative. When they run out of words, young children supplement with body language. Partnership with parents is important to enable you to fill in the gaps. Two-year-olds may want to tell you something interesting about their home life, or to tell their parents about an important event at nursery or with their childminder. Twos, who are confident of the interest and time of their important adults, will also sometimes request the retelling of a personal narrative – out of interest and sometimes to lay to rest less happy events.

For example

- At nearly two, Drew wanted to tell me about his day with his childminder. Something important had happened that he explained with, 'No Diane – so sad.' Drew's childminder was called Angela, so I was perplexed. I asked, 'Who's Diane?' and 'What was so sad?'. Drew tried but could only emphasise that there had been, 'No Diane' and that was definitely 'sad'. I asked Angela the following day who explained that Diane usually came to their street every Tuesday and sold fruit and vegetables out of the back of her van. Drew looked forward to this weekly event of choosing produce from Diane and having a chat with her.
- At two years three months, Drew clearly recalled our trip to a zoo. Several times within the following weeks Drew said firmly, 'went zoo' and looked at me expectantly. He wanted a retelling of our outing and he joined in the narrative where he was able.
- At two years eight months, Drew's request for me to recount a narrative arose from an incident that had worried him. His baby sister's crying had been so persistent one night that she had woken Drew. He

Being a helpful adult

Rising twos and two-year-olds really are skilful communicators. But those skills are not promoted by plastic toys and electronic, so-called learning systems.

Some toys flagged as suitable for two-year-olds, even babies, are covered with letters and numbers, along with glaring primary colours. A bus or toy telephone is ruined for genuine pretend play; a potentially useful soft toy is turned into visual overload. Resist such toys - they are not 'good value' because they have so much jammed onto the surface. Nor do they teach phonics to young children – no matter what it says on the packet or manual!

There is a genuine risk of over-stimulation for young children, if they are surrounded by toys that are visually so busy. Many are also overloaded with sound. The pressure of a finger releases a voice that allegedly 'teaches your child' shapes or random words.

Young children learn neither vocabulary nor abstract concepts in this manner; they need real people and real conversation in context.

Babies and young children do not learn from the disembodied voice of a stranger powered by batteries.

came to find me, concerned to ask, 'Are you crying Mama?' In the next few weeks Drew asked me several times, 'Talk about the dark'. He wanted to go through the narrative from when he heard the crying, how he got out of his bed in the dark, through to the happy resolution that it was not me crying at all, but the 'noisy' baby. Less than a year and a half later, the noisy baby was herself able to initiate a conversation about past events.

- Tanith, at one year 11 months, used the phrase 'balloon bang' to recall and have retold the narrative of how the Hallowe'en balloon had burst the previous week and everyone had jumped.
- At two years one month, she recalled in the late afternoon, 'Drew cake rip it' – a reference to how that morning Drew had energetically torn up his picture of a cake.
- At two years two months, Tanith said, 'Baby Anna Christmas' to recall and talk about the interesting visit for the Christmas period by our friends, who had brought their six-week-old baby.
- By two years six months, Tanith enjoyed creating a narrative herself by combining bits of familiar stories that I told out loud and her favourite story books

Talking and listening with young children

Speech and language teams have become increasingly concerned about the fragile communication skills of many three- to five-year-olds. Primary school teams comment on how five- and six-year-olds seem to struggle to hold a conversation or listen well enough to cope with classroom life.

Problems seem to have arisen, for some individuals and group teams, when adults feel under pressure to meet targets and gather evidence. They feel there is no time to spend (or waste) in what appears to be idle chit-chat with children. The consequences can be serious for young children's language development. This section describes some of the key issues about getting practitioners, and parents, back on track. But you will find more material in other books in this series, for instance in *What Does it Mean to be Four?* (page 28)

Children learn about words, sentence structure and use of language through relaxed, one-to-one interactions with friendly, familiar adults. If they receive appropriate personal attention, then children do not need special language programmes, unless they have specific communication difficulties. However, some of the practical ideas in this section would be appropriate for you to support threes and fours whose language appears to be delayed. Try the simple approaches first, unless there is already reason to suppose that a known disability is affecting a child's skills of communication.

For example

Young children are generally interested in conversation. They enjoy and want to have conversations with adults who are attentive and follow the flow of children's interest.

During the day I spent at St Mark's Nursery School, one of the practitioners split her sandal. The children were interested and I heard a mix of twos, threes and fours chat with her in a sustained conversation. They wanted to know what had happened, why she was barefoot (she had taken the sandals off in the garden), what she was going to do now and when she went home. One child wondered whether she really liked the sandals. The children sounded interested in whether this adult was upset that her sandal was beyond repair. The practitioner did like the sandals, so then children wanted to know, would she buy another pair exactly the same and, if so, where?

The questions kept coming and the practitioner answered each question patiently and with good humour. It was a good example of an adult being available for children and going with the flow of what had caught their attention. There was no way an incident like this could have been planned. The planning element is that in St Mark's practitioners are attentive and available to children.

Practitioners and parents need to hold tight, or return, to basic adult communication skills and personal attention that help young children to strengthen as skilful communicators. What works best of all is actually very simple - not complicated 'communication techniques'! If practitioners are to be helpful to young children, sometimes you have to recognise what seems to stop you talking and listening – what blocks sensible adult behaviour?

You will help two-year-olds to develop and feel confident in their skills of communication when you behave in the following ways.

- Be close to young children; the social basis to conversation does not get established over distance. Young children will show you what is their comfortable, personal space, but certainly you need to be close enough to touch. An early years practitioner commented to me that, in her own training, she was told that any small group with young children should be small enough that you can stretch out and touch each child.
- Get and stay on a child's level and make friendly eye contact. When you are chatting and listening to several young children, perhaps sitting indoors on a sofa or outdoors on a seat or grass, let your eyes tell each child in turn 'I'm listening to you; I'm interested in what you're telling me.'
- You need to look and sound interested in children's play and interests. Use facial expression and tone to show you enjoy chatting with this child. Your intonation can be rather more expressive than you might use with a fellow adult.
- A slower, more musical intonation can get and hold the attention of young children whose communication skills are under-developed – either through limited experience or for a language disability that may become clear later.
- When you start a conversation, or want to make a suggestion or request, make sure you have a child's attention. Say a child's name at the beginning of your phrase; do not leave it to the end. If a two-year-old (or threes as well) are busy, then they may not realise you are talking to them, until they hear their own name. You can also use gentle touch, eye contact or a direct smile.
- Music is an excellent addition to the day, but use it selectively, so that children start to recognise pieces of music and songs. Continuous background music is not stimulating; it becomes sound wallpaper that is no longer appreciated. It takes children's energy to filter it out of their awareness.
- Some group provision, especially those that operate in one large room, can have problems with noise level. It is really worth looking at your use of space and creating smaller, comfortable indoor spaces that encourage peaceful interaction.

Communication has a strong social underpinning and proper conversation has give-and-take. You can show conversational skills in action by how you behave with children.

- Show young children what a good listener looks like. Pay attention, ask for a repeat or simple explanation, if you do not understand. Make your comments link with what a young child has just told you. If you have reason to change the direction of the conversation then flag that up, perhaps with, 'Can I tell you about...?' or 'That reminds me of....'
- Keep it simple and use short phrases that enable two-year-olds to take in

Being a helpful adult

Of course you talk, as your contribution to the conversation. But non-stop adult talk is overwhelming for twos – and for threes and fours.

- Young children need time to process what you have said and then to process their response. The gaps may be longer than conversations with slightly older children.
- Respect and use the power of the pause.
- You can comment gently, 'You're thinking' or 'Are you still thinking?'
- If you rush to fill the silence, you risk disrupting concentration. You will also fill the gap by guessing what the child wants to say or adding another question or comment while the child is still working on your earlier remark.
- If a child remains silent or looks perplexed in response to, 'Are you still busy thinking?' then you can ask, 'Did you hear what I said?' or 'Did you understand what I asked? Am I making sense?'
- You can model 'thinking time' for children. For example, you might say after a short pause of your own, 'That's a tricky question. I'm thinking about my answer. Right, what I'd say is...' or 'Let me think about that. Now how did we build the castle last time?'

Being a helpful adult

The best approach is to ask children questions when you genuinely want to know the answer. Avoid testing questions to check if a child knows names, colours and so on.

When you spend time close to young children in play and conversation, you will find out easily enough what they understand by watching and listening to them.

Twos often enjoy spotting games led by 'Where's the...?' or 'Who can find me something that is...?' supported by body language when your gestures will add meaning to words like 'little' or 'soft'.

When adults – parents as well as practitioners - are concerned about a child's language development, they often increase their questioning. If young children do not understand you in the first place, then more questions do not help. In fact, the barrage is more likely to make a child feel under greater pressure to respond correctly. It is far better to adjust how you talk to make a simple comment as your contribution, pause and look expectant.

what you say, one manageable chunk at a time. The younger twos feel overloaded if your sentences roll on or several requests are bundled up in one long sentence.

- By all means say a word correctly back to a child, as part of your extension in reply. But do not make children re-say a word or phrase, as this feels like unpleasant pressure. They will listen and reform their words and sentence construction in line with what you say.
- It works well to use a child's own words and add a bit or slightly rephrase. For instance, a child says, 'It go there' and, because you are close and attentive, you can sensibly say, 'Yes, our bricks go into the big box. Well done.'
- When you introduce a topic of conversation or what could be a new idea, then make sure that young children have a good chance of grasping your meaning. You might say, 'I can hear the birds singing' but at the same time you point to those birds in the tree.

Questions are fine, when....

The 'Talking Time' research, led by Julie Dockrell (see Resources, page 52), focused in particular on how language models, provided by adults but also peers, exert a significant influence on how children develop their oral language skills. In training sessions with staff, 'The importance of adult recasts of children's utterances and the drawing of appropriate contrasts between words and grammatical constructions were highlighted. The importance of retaining the child's basic meaning was seen as central to such activities. Staff were encouraged to avoid direct questions and demands, following an inflexible script or forcing the child to repeat what was said.' (page 6, report on the Literacy Trust website)

Questions have their place within social conversation, but questioning can be overdone, until it feels like cross-questioning. In *Foundations of Literacy*, Sue Palmer and Ros Bayley (see Resources, page 52) comment that, 'One type of questioning that is often successful...is a display of genuine curiosity. Rather than asking questions like a teacher, ask them like an equal, for instance, asking children how they did something or asking for their help. This less direct, social questioning shows that you are interested in and respect their ideas'.

Helpful adults encourage two-year-olds to ask their own questions, because they show genuine interest and answer the questions. So, listen to children's questions and persevere when you are not quite sure what they are asking. Their questions tell you what they want to puzzle out – a far better route for young learning than adults following their own agenda of what they want children to know. Then the twos develop into enquiring threes and knowledgeable fours, who have a good sense of what they do not understand. (See for instance, *What Does it Mean to be Three?* page 26, and *What Does it Mean to be Four?* page 25)

The importance of talking out loud

Talking out loud helps young children to link thought and action. Many young children voice their thoughts and comment on their actions without having to be encouraged. Watch twos as they play in the sand or work with playdough. They often say, 'Need more' or 'Put it here'. Helpful adults treat a child's self talk as interesting. You can help and listen to young children as you play alongside them, or are engaged in domestic routines like tidying upt. Never tell them to be quiet.

It is helpful to young children when you voice your own thinking process. You do not have to sound unhinged when you behave in this way! Young children regard self talk as perfectly natural. So, you might be in the block corner with a child and say, 'I think I'll make a bridge', pause, then add 'I'm going to need some more bricks' (you might ask if the child can spare some). 'Now I've built the sides of my bridge. I need a long block to lay over them.' You might use a combination of comments on your actions and those of a child helper, if you were organising a snack or drinks together.

For example

The *Key Times* video (see Resources - page 53) has several sequences that show how an involved practitioner can comment appropriately. One observation sequence related to the section on communication skills shows a practitioner in a nursery home corner with several young children. She comments appropriately on what children have in their hands or what they are doing. The practitioner is generous with her gestures to support the communication, especially since several children are in the process of learning English as an additional language.

Later in the video the same practitioner is close to two children who are absorbed at the water tray with clear tubes and corks. The practitioner watches with interest and comments in a simple way about how the tubes are filled by children pouring water and how the corks come up to the top.

In the *Birth to Three Matters* video you can hear and see many examples of where an attentive practitioner voices what is happening or puts into words what a child has indicated by gesture, for instance, in outdoors sequences, around the meal table or in the friendly care sequence when a toddler has their nappy changed.

Several of the video excerpts on the *Birth to Three Matters* CD-Rom also show a supportive practitioner putting thoughts into words and describing actions out loud. Look at the sequence of feeding the guinea pigs (under each aspect of 'A healthy child') and a young child with what looks like her childminder, playing with picture cards (under 'A skilful communicator', 'Finding a voice').

Can you help with small groups?

The 'Talking Time' research project, led by Julie Dockrell at the Institute of Education in London, supported several inner-city nursery classes to establish a regular small group session called talking time. The intervention was launched because of concerns about the children's communication skills. Language assessment established that the children (with an average age of three years six months at the beginning of the project) were significantly delayed in their verbal language skills, although not their non-verbal.

Observation in nurseries showed that the children had limited experience within their day to hear adults speak. The impression given in the report is that many of the staff did not interact much with children when they were engaged in free play indoors or outside. Talk that might encourage language development occurred mainly in small group activities for the children and structured teaching activities. There was considerable variation, but in some nurseries the researchers observed no time on activities that they judged would enhance oral language development.

There seemed to be two problems: some staff did not really understand the importance of oral language skills; and the high sense of pressure to meet targets. The 'Talking Time' team maintained a regular presence in the nurseries, realising that, 'The staff found it difficult to programme the activities and considerable

Food for thought

The 'Talking Time', and some other research projects (Julie Dockrell - see Resources, page 52), often work with a group format for language intervention. These are small groups – the 'Talking Time' project specified a maximum of five children - but communication is nevertheless within a group. This approach takes as a given that nurseries and other group settings will work a lot with young children in groups.

Local speech and language teams are advising group practitioners to hold more conversations with individual children or very small groups that children themselves have formed. Three-year-olds are usually the youngest involved in research projects like 'Talking Time' and they clearly need personal attention. Twos are increasingly likely to be in group settings. Some teams therefore need to rethink their approach: all communication does not happen in a group format and through adult-planned activities to support communication.

The Effective Provision of Pre-school Education (EPPE) research (see page 53) stressed that the most effective settings had practitioners who came alongside children in their chosen activities. When an experience arose from an adult-initiated activity, it was then important that children had plenty of scope to explore and discuss. What the EPPE team called 'sustained shared thinking' then happened when the adults watched, listened and added their communication in many of the ways described on page 33.

amounts of external training and support were required' (page 14). This monitoring seems to have avoided the problem that occurred in a Sheffield study (described in *What Does it Mean to be Four?* page 28) when some nurseries committed to join a special language intervention project, yet perceived time pressures meant that the programme was run in a much reduced version.

Nevertheless, the sense of pressure remains. The 'Talking Time' research found that the nurseries were prepared to continue the special small group sessions once the study was finished. However, the programme was reduced from twice a week to only one session. The research team's judgement was that once a week would not be enough to support children in the ways they needed, given their delayed language skills.

Social communication between children

Many children gain a sibling when they are two. So a continuing relationship with a younger child is part of normal life for many twos and young threes. Georgia (described by Cath Arnold in *Observing Harry* - see Resources, page 52) was two years three months when Harry was born. Alice (described by Robin Campbell in *Literacy from Home to School: Reading with Alice* - see Resources, page 52)) gained baby sister Caitlin three weeks before Alice's second birthday. Drew gained his baby sister Tanith three days before his second birthday. The diaries kept of each of these young children show that the new sibling was important and his or her presence led to lines of conversation including questions. Younger siblings bring some annoyance, but in each case the older child brought their brother or sister alongside to join in play that the younger one would not have managed alone.

For example

Ishbel (part of the Baby it's You group - see Resources, page 52) at two years three months is eating an ice cream with her mother and younger brother Duncan. The conversational flow shows well what a young two-year-old can manage. Ishbel's mother helps with the communication in a friendly way when, at the end, Ishbel runs out of words.

Mother: How does it make you feel when you eat it?

Ishbel: Cold!

Mother: Do you think it makes him feel cold?

Ishbel: It's cold because it's been in the freezer.

Mother: Oh oh!

Ishbel: He's ripped the tag.

(Ishbel starts to talk about rabbits.)

Mother: Is Duncan a rabbit?

Ishbel: No, he's gonna be a tiger mask.

Mother: So he's gonna wear a tiger mask, is he? I think I'd better clean him. Tell him to be careful.

Ishbel: Be careful Dunky. If you do that you'll be crying and then your mother has to put…er…up and don't ever do it again.

Mother: Did you get that, Duncan? Ishbel was telling you not to lean back in the high chair.

(Page 199-200)

Being a helpful adult

Early years practitioners need to be secure in their knowledge of child development. The 'Talking Time' research highlighted that some staff were shaky in their knowledge of young language development, their ability to make accurate observations of children's language or both.

- 54 per cent of the staff interviewed stated that between a half and three quarters of the children entering their nursery had a 'good knowledge of language'. This belief contrasted with the language assessment that placed 90 per cent of the children as below average in their language skills and over half significantly delayed. The children's average non-verbal skills were within the normal range for their age.
- Most staff did not have the language skills themselves to judge children in their home language (when it was not English). However, they nevertheless felt confident to state that those children had good language skills in their home language.
- A third of the staff 'felt that "watching television by themselves can be useful in developing children's spoken language" (page 9). Since this statement is developmentally unsound, the staff confidence in such a view is worrying.

In a relaxed atmosphere two-year-olds develop friendships with their age peers, or with slightly older children. They need a predictable pattern of attendance in out-of-home care, if such friendships are to develop. Very flexible and changing patterns may suit parents, or enable settings (and politicians!) to claim that such arrangements are meeting the demands of working parents. But a two-year-old cocktail party circuit does not enable the familiarity, shared games and interests that are necessary for friendship to flourish. Two-year-olds sometimes play in parallel, but if you watch them, you will see that they are often attentive to what is going on alongside. They often make a friendly move, play and chat together.

For example

- Look at the *Birth to Three Matters* video excerpt on the CD-Rom, under 'Listening and responding'. A sequence shows two children sitting happily together with their books. They chat and look at one another's book. The boy has an 'Incy Wincy Spider' book and he says the rhyme to his companion. She joins in with the hand movements.
- At Windham Parent and Toddler Drop-in I watched three two-year-olds at the water tray. They worked busily with the water and the available equipment. Sometimes they paused and watched each other – with interest and concentration. They managed because there were enough resources and adults were close by should they need any help.
- Sometimes young children like to play alone for a while. In Windham I watched a two-year-old girl playing absorbed for ten minutes in the play kitchen – putting items in and out of the toy oven then in and out again. She was later joined by another child and then together they spent time posting a plastic knife through the oven door, seeing what happened, retrieving it and posting it again.

For example

Communication can happen between young friends even when one partner is much younger or when one child has a disability that affects communication. Both examples are from the section on 'The interest in developing social relationships with their peers' from the *Key Times* file (see Resources, page 53).

- Jamib, aged two years ten months, has moderate to severe hearing loss and had been fitted with his first hearing aid. He enjoys trying out different sounds but is not yet able to form recognisable words. He likes to join in the meal table conversation and makes a sound to his friend seated next to him. The friend repeats the sound back and the two children repeat that sound to and fro, looking at each other and laughing together.

- Taylor (three years) and Jonathan (two years) are playing together, exploring cornflour. Taylor buries both hands in the cornflour and says, 'It's sticky'. Jonathan watches the older boy closely, imitates his actions and then his words with, 'sticky'. Taylor says, 'It's cold' and Jonathan says, 'Cold ooh'. Taylor says, 'Where have my fingers gone?' and Jonathan echoes, 'Finger gone'. Taylor then says, 'It's funny' and Jonathan is ready with, 'funny' and laughs. Taylor covers his hands with cornflour and Jonathan imitates him again.

This example shows the value of ensuring that younger children mix with older ones. Flexible materials like cornflour are suitable for twos and threes. Taylor probably enjoyed taking the lead and Jonathan had a lot of fun imitating.

Being a helpful adult

Television or video can have a useful place in the daily life of two-year-olds but must be used with care. You will support children if you:

- Choose only those programmes that are appropriate for twos and switch the television off when the programme has finished.
- Watch with children, so you can listen to their comments and make brief comments yourself if appropriate - but do not talk over the interesting bits
- Use age-appropriate videos and let them become familiar to the twos, without constant watching.

The problem with excessive television, and programmes that are not age-appropriate, is that the medium is non-interactive. Despite technological advances, television is still a screen. There is a lack of social connection for young children since, even if they reply to the people on the screen, the programme continues regardless of what the child has said.

Twos need to hear language that is linked with actions and real objects in front of them. They also need more pauses for thought than are offered by the more frenetic programmes.

You can find useful information in a review by Robin Close, *Television and language development in the early years: a review of the literature* for the Literacy Trust (www.literacytrust.co.uk)

Being a helpful adult

Some twos are learning more than one language - either simultaneously or one language following on after they have started to grasp the first. It is possible that two-year-olds may be slightly slower than average in each language if they are learning two languages at the same time. But looked at logically, children have probably taken on as much language knowledge as their monolingual peers.

You can help by using the supportive approach outlined on page 21. Young children with whom you do not share a fluent language will nevertheless be thinking like two-year-olds. You help by linking your words and short phrases directly to what you are doing, the child is doing or what is in front of you both. Then twos can make a connection of meaning for your spoken words.

Everyone needs to recognise and respect what these twos can manage. What you do not do is to pronounce that twos have 'no language', just because they speak a home language that you do not understand.

Social skills and problem-solving

A positive approach to supporting the behaviour of any young children has to be firmly grounded in realistic expectations. Everyone has to consider what young twos can genuinely manage in terms of turn taking. What kinds of sharing are too much to expect, even from the older twos, especially if an adult is not alongside as back-up diplomat and calm negotiator?

Parents and early years practitioners help when they tune in to the current position taken by very young children and guide them on from there. We do not help by constantly telling them 'You must share' – or other kinds of nagging. Adults need to make sure that there are plenty of favourite resources and this approach usually means providing flexible materials rather than separate toys.

Two-year-olds respond well to the visual message of 'plenty for everyone' when they can see lots of building blocks, plenty of dressing-up hats and bags or loads of dolly pegs and containers. Then you will often see twos spontaneously offer items to their peers. Sometimes the actions are within a game of 'I give it to you and then you give it back again' but on other occasions the behaviour seems to be motivated by a genuine 'You need some and I've got enough to spare'.

Solving problems

Even with plenty of resources and supportive adults, a two-year-old's social skills will sometimes be exhausted and the emotional temperature will soar, along with the noise level. As hard as it may feel, the only way to help children is to show them the kind of problem-solving skills that you would like them to learn. If you are to help two-year-olds with such skills, then you have to understand and use problem-solving skills yourself, and that means committing the time.

The High/Scope approach to conflict resolution took the key points from adult problem-solving and conflict resolution and adjusted them for use, even with very young children. This section describes the main issues and the approach is relevant up the age range (see also *What Does it Mean to be Four?* page 15)
You can see these skills in action with two-year-olds in two High/Scope videos: *It's mine! Responding to Problems and Conflicts* and the conflict resolution section of *The High/Scope Approach to Under-Threes.* There are also many written examples in Betsy Evans' *You Can't Come to my Birthday Party!* (see Resources, page 52)

Even in well-organised nurseries, or homes for that matter, young children sometimes resort to raised voices, or worse when they both want the same cuddly toy or chair. Two-year-old power of language means that even friends may fall out over whether the vehicle in front of them is called a car or a truck. Two-year-olds will not manage the talking through that can become possible, with experience and practice, for four-year-olds. But supportive, and patient adults, lay the ground work by calmly shifting a verbal or physical argument into a problem-solving exchange. The steps are as follows:

Step 1: Approach swiftly and calm the situation

If you are not already close, move to the children. Use firm but gentle physical contact to stop any hurtful behaviour between the children. You need to be close and at two-year-old eye level. Be calm and, if you have to raise your voice slightly to get their attention, then come back swiftly to normal volume.

Step 2: Acknowledge children's feelings

Make simple statements like, 'You look cross' or 'Yes, I can hear that you're upset'. Two-year-olds, especially young twos, will not have the words to express emotions, so you can help by providing words to name the feelings and to say what is happening.

Step 3: Be open to information from the children

Young twos are unlikely to be able to answer the question, 'What has happened?' But you help by saying, 'Let's see what's going on here'. As older twos become more able to speak up, then you show that you are fair and listen to all sides.

Step 4: Acknowledge that there is a problem

It helps children when you turn a situation from being a quarrel to a problem that needs solving. You can use a phrase like, 'We have a problem here' and then use simple words to describe what is happening like, 'You want the bike and he wants the bike too'. When the dispute is over an item, then it is useful either to explain that you will take care of the car or doll for the time being. If young children cannot bring themselves to let go, or the item is large, then it can work well for everyone, including you, to keep one hand on the item.

Step 5: Invite and offer solutions

Your words and calming body language all communicate, 'What can we do to solve this problem?' You do not get embroiled in who had it first. Young twos may not be able to offer a way out, so you will need to offer: 'I have an idea. Would you like to hear my idea?' You then suggest a way out that could resolve the situation without one child really being a winner and the other a loser.

Step 6: Be prepared to give follow-up support

Two-year-olds who have become emotional are likely to need you to stay close by to ease them back into happy play or conversation. However, it can happen that your calming approach brings down the emotional temperature quickly.

Using these skills of conflict resolution takes time, adult patience and commitment. It can seem quicker to step in and sort everything out as if you know who had it first or announce that with all this noise nobody can have the bike! But in the long run, this quick-fix approach does not support young children to resolve their own problems. In the short run, they will soon say that you are 'unfair' and 'never listen'. If you want competent young children then you have to put in the time.

Food for thought

Two-year-old social skills are work in progress. My thanks to the Windham Parent Toddler drop-in for 'The Property Laws of the Toddler', which they provide as an amusing, yet accurate, reminder.

- If I like it, it's mine.
- If it's in my hand, it's mine.
- If I can take it from you, it's mine.
- If it's mine, it must never appear to be yours, in any way.
- If I had it a little while ago, it's mine.
- If I'm doing or building something, all the pieces are mine.
- If it looks just like mine, it's mine.
- If I think it's mine, it's mine.

You help to modify the 'property laws' when you are close by, watch, listen and intervene as a good natured diplomat before the crisis explodes.

Attentive and aware adults can contribute a level of negotiation skills that are beyond two-year-olds, unless they have some kindly support.

A competent learner

How do you best support very young learners?

The eighth and ninth principles in the *Birth to Three Matters* introduction booklet are:

- **Children learn when they are given appropriate responsibility, allowed to make errors, decisions and choices, and respected as autonomous and competent learners.**
- **Children learn by doing rather than being told.**

The Effective Provision of Pre-school Education (EPPE) project started with more than 3,000 three-year-olds in England and followed them to their Key Stage 1 SATs. The project has detailed how a good quality early years group experience can support young children's learning and make a noticeable difference to those children whose social background is likely to put them at an educational disadvantage.

The Researching Effective Pedagogy in the Early Years (REPEY) project followed up some of the most effective settings identified from the EPPE project and also emphasised that any old pre-school experience does not bring about these positive changes for young children.

- Children were shown to benefit from starting in a good quality early years setting from two years of age. But the most effective settings were those that combined care and early education.
- The EPPE project highlighted the significance of family, shared activities such as enjoying books together, singing and rhymes, painting and drawing, local visits including to the library and regular opportunities for children to have friends to play with.
- Quality was dependent on how practitioners behaved towards children. Warm interactive relationships were crucial – young children needed to feel at ease to benefit from the learning environment.
- Adults are active in planning opportunities, but do not set out to control how children use play materials or engage in activities. The best settings were those in which children chose their own activities for about half the time and came alongside practitioners in adult-initiated activities for the other half.
- There is nothing in the research to recommend that this 50-50 split is managed in a structured way. So long as adults have used their planning skills to create an interesting and easily accessible learning environment, then children are able to decide what they want to do and move at their own pace between areas of interest.

Following the flow

Once twos have become familiar with an inviting, appropriately resourced learning environment, they will move around at their own pace. They focus on what interests them today. When two-year-olds feel confident that adult attention is there for the asking, they do not have to keep checking on your availability.

For example

- Two-year-old Gary moved around the Windham drop-in with confidence. Sometimes his mother was close by, sometimes he was absorbed in play and she was across the room. Gary moved between the opportunities that were available. He spent some time with the mark-making materials set out on a table. He was equally interested to explore letting a wheeled toy run down a slope to his mother. He spent time emptying a container of keys, exploring many of them individually – looking and feeling.
- Young children learn a great deal through play but they do not only learn through activities that adults would usually label as 'play'. Twos, just like threes to fives, are keen to be involved in familiar routines. They warm to feeling like a trusted helper and genuinely learn from being part of organising a snack or preparing food for pets (see the example on page 46 about feeding the guinea pigs).

The research review, undertaken by Colwyn Trevarthen to support the Scottish *Birth to Three*, emphasises the importance of playful adult companionship. However, the review recognises that toddlers and twos become more and more able to play together. It says: 'Young children need attuned adult companionship more than older ones and childcare settings need to be planned, and staff trained, to assure that this is normally available. Research has shown that children under three generally play more easily and with more creativity with mothers or caregivers than with peers, but toddlers in their second year, who know each other, can elaborate creative play with age-mates and these capacities develop rapidly.' (page 30)

For example

Twos often play alongside each other but there should never be any sense that parallel play is inferior. Children who are close together using the same source of materials often watch each other.

Being a helpful adult

Young children's schemas will come alive to you when you take the time to look, listen and note. Carmel Brennan (*The Power of Play*, see Resources page 52) shows how photographs and noting a simple narrative line captures the power of play. Genuine learning can be overlooked when observation follows an activity, and anticipated learning outcome, planned tightly by the adults.

Two practitioners share their insights from this kind of record keeping. Teresa has captured on camera how one young boy concentrated on his current schema of lining things up. Her open-ended observation has shown: 'Here's Laura painting – she shows her painting to teacher but as soon as teacher leaves, she starts painting her hand. That's what she really wanted to do. She was only doing what the teacher wants while she was around.'

Even observant, familiar adults still make an informed guess about the plans and motivation of very young children. Cath Arnold, who describes Harry's absorbing interest in connection, is his grandmother as well as an experienced early years practitioner (*Observing Harry* - see Resources, page 52). But she still does not always know exactly what Harry has in mind – the whys and wherefores of his actions.

- Several examples in Carmel Brennan's *The Power of Play* (see Resources, page 52) show how children observe each other - sometimes without exchanging a word. For instance, Dillon (page 48) is struggling to blow bubbles. But he watches the child next to him, can see the technique and now manages it successfully.
- Twos and toddlers, who know each other, can play together in sustained sequences. In Windham drop-in, Jamie and Sara (both two-year-olds) chose to play together most of the session. Jamie's mother explained that they were close friends and regularly played together in each other's family homes. At the drop-in, their current play choice was to get a wheeled wooden carriage each, put a dolly or teddy in each one and then wheel them about in tandem on the outdoor decking area. They would stop from time to time, line themselves up on two outdoor seats, park the buggies and take out the dolls for a cuddle. They sat like that for a while, had a chat and looked at each other's dollies, then put the dolls back and headed off again for another walk. They were completely absorbed and happily at ease with each other. At one point the wheels of the buggies locked with one buggy pointing forwards and the other backwards. The two children continued to walk, going 'beep-beep', although Jamie had to walk backwards.

Method in apparent mess

Problems can arise when practitioners or parents require a neat form of play or use of resource materials. Absorbed twos do not necessarily follow the track of exploration that unreflective adults might think of as 'proper play'. The idea of observing schemas is a useful way to tune into young children.

Chris Athey developed Jean Piaget's idea of schemas and her practical application of the approach has encouraged flexible, observation-led practice. The work of the Pen Green Centre in Corby is probably best known, as a result of Cath Arnold's accounts of Georgia and Harry. You can find a short summary in the *Birth to Three Matters* CD-Rom under 'Making Connections'. When you observe a persistent pattern of playful exploration for an individual child it is described as a schema. Their current schema shapes what they do with resources, including their own body, over a period of time. There is flexibility in their play – schemas do not indicate rigid repetition – but twos who are fascinated by rotation or connection, for example, can be persistent.

For example

- Carmel Brennan describes Ali, a girl who persistently used a schema of enveloping. Words and photographs (in *The Power of Play*) show how Ali spent time wrapping up her dolls with great care. But she was also keen to use other materials to wrap presents for her friends.
- Carmel Brennan also describes Martin, who is absorbed in filling bags and moving materials around his playgroup. Part of his play is as a customer in the shop corner. But Martin's interest in filling bags and transporting materials around the setting extends beyond the shop role play.

Young children sometimes spend a relatively brief time wrapping items or carrying them about their home or nursery. You would not suggest that they have an enveloping or transporting schema unless they continue to show this absorbing interest. One afternoon in a nursery I watched a toddler spend a lot of time looking through her own legs. That day she seemed fascinated by how the world looked upside down. But observation over more than one day would be needed to decide whether she was exploring a schema around relative position and orientation. A single afternoon was not enough to know.

A schema does not dominate all playful interaction. Two-year-olds, who are currently intrigued by enclosure, will spend time building cotton-reel fences for the dinosaurs or experiment with lines and borders to enclose some of their paintings. But they will play in other ways as well.

The *Birth to Three Matters* pack includes the idea of schemas to encourage adults to create an accessible learning environment and discourage rigid, pre-planned activities. Two-year-olds – and threes and fours – need to spread out and have access to flexible play resources. Then young children currently absorbed by connection can link items together using glue or string, connect items by using building blocks or choose from generous mark-making materials to connect on paper or card.

Learning about abstract ideas

Two-year-olds are likely to have a large vocabulary, including some words that describe qualities like texture, weight, temperature or colour. However, they reach this understanding through practical experience, when the words can be connected with something that already makes sense.

Ideas that seem obvious to adults, because we have lived with them for so long, are not at all obvious to young children. You will tune in properly to two-year-olds, if you consider how they could experience different abstract ideas through one or more of their senses. How does an idea come alive? For example:

- **Vision:** young children need to use sight to recognise and distinguish different colour and shades. They have to see the difference before they can assign a word to that colour. When the day closes in swiftly during wintertime, two-year-olds can see the difference between light and dark and how adults need to put the light on.
- **Touch:** children need to feel textures like rough, smooth, bumpy (which could also be experienced by riding over) and some temperature changes like warm, hot or cold. As well as seeing basic shapes and lines, young children often learn by feeling the curves of a ball or cylinder or the edges of a squared box.
- **Hearing:** children distinguish levels of volume with loud, noisy and quiet.
- **Taste:** they use the power of taste not only for nice and nasty, but to appreciate some of the subtle flavours of food and drink with tasty, crunchy or juicy. They also often have their own words like the nearly two-year-old (told to me) who used the word 'nippy' to cover sharp or sour tastes like lemon.
- **Smell:** probably the most overlooked sense but important to young children who recognise a whole concept of 'smells like...' but then possibly do not get much further than variations around nice and nasty, because adults do not have many concept words for fragrances.
- Elinor Goldschmied highlighted a 'sixth sense' when she described her practical ideas of the treasure basket and exploratory play in *People under Three: Young Children in Day Care* (Routledge, chapter 6). She was talking about the messages that children need to notice from their own body. The terms proprioception or kinesthetic feedback refer to a similar concept. Young children may use sight to look up for a sense of 'high' but climbing up high or stretching up for something on a high shelf gives another dimension to their understanding. Cars can be seen to go fast on the road or a child can make a toy truck speed along the paving.

Food for thought

Twos – and threes for that matter – do not 'learn their colours' more effectively by having their environment colour coded.

If they are tuned into colour already, twos do not need you messing about with their interest table, replacing everything with yellow items.

If they are currently busy grappling with wet and dry, they do not want you to give their water tray an attack of jaundice. They want to be able to mix water with the sand or have a supply of items that you will let them drop into the water tray and see what happens.

Used with care, a topic approach to early learning can work within the Foundation Stage. However, it becomes developmentally unstable with young threes and under threes. Their general knowledge and thinking processes do not work in this way. It is therefore regrettable that the *Birth to Three Matters* team chose to put the example of a topic on 'Edges' into the CD-Rom, label it 'Planning' and attach it to every component. This approach does not fit anything else about planning and resourcing on the cards, nor any features written by team members (that I have encountered).

But there is another level of understanding when a two- or three-year-old whooshes fast down the slide or runs from one end of the garden to another.

When you watch and listen, you realise that nearly twos and twos learn first those concepts that are of direct interest and relevance to them. Young climbers may easily grasp 'high' or 'high up'. Drew at just two years of age had a clear concept of 'too high' – as in 'too high wall' – an accurate judgement of local walls that I would say were 'too high' for him to walk along holding my hand. Keen transporters and block builders may soon make sense of 'heavy'. Young children who love their food have reason to learn 'tasty' or 'crunchy'. Twos may understand the difference between 'hot' and 'cold' linked with their meal or related to the weather.

There is no sound developmental reason for the emphasis on colour and shape in many nurseries. These two concepts dominate topic books and plastic toys. We want to support young children as they make the move into abstract thinking. It does not matter which ideas come first, so long as we recognise that exciting move into being able to describe the world, as well as name objects and actions.

Colour and shape are complicated concepts. The two words are general, umbrella terms that then encompass all the specific descriptive words like 'red' or 'blue', 'round' or 'square'. Twos learn about these concepts in the same way as any other ideas – by having the word linked with something of relevance and interest that is in front of them. They do not learn better or faster when settings feel that they have to have a colour and shape of the week. I have encountered this developmentally unsound approach even in toddler rooms.

Twos learn about colours when adults link the colour word to items of clothing or play resources that a child really likes: 'Paresh, you're got your red wellingtons on today. Those are my favourites.' My own daughter locked onto pink first, because her favourite bike at drop-in was a lurid shade of pink. It made sense for me to say, 'The pink bike is free, off you go!'

Making sense of descriptive words

Toddlers and very young children learn about abstract concepts through a considerable amount of varied experience and hands-on exploration of their world. They need to connect words that stand for ideas to what they experience through their senses.

- When a child is playing with a set of dolls there could be good reason to say, 'Yes, you've got the large doll not the tiny one.'
- Helpful adults drop the words into their communication at a time and place that gives direct meaning. You might say, 'The dolls' clothes are really wet. Perhaps we had better squeeze them before we hang them on the line'.
- Twos, even young threes, need to be able to connect what you say with something that makes sense to them. You help by listening and then following the child's lead with, 'Yes, look at that water! It's going down the drain so fast'. Or you comment on what the child is doing: 'You're building such a tall tower'.
- The concept of opposites only seems obvious to adults because you have lived with pairs like wet/dry or hot/cold for a long time. Two-year-olds usually get one half of an opposite at a time, like big and little, and then, if they are interested, they may go for fine gradations such as very big and tiny.
- Young children even start to grasp the idea of emotions if you use feelings words, like happy or curious, in a context that gives them meaning to the child. You can expand a little on what young twos have just said, like 'Daddy bye work'. You need to know the child well, listen and look at her face to make a good guess about whether it is appropriate to say, 'Yes, your Daddy went to work didn't he? And you gave him such a big hug goodbye'. Or perhaps her face leads you to say, 'Yes, you said bye-bye to Daddy didn't you. Do you miss him? You look a little bit sad.'

What does early literacy look like?

Two-year-olds, supported by genuinely helpful adults, can be building a strong basis for literacy. Developmentally sound early literacy is created when:

- Very young children are enthusiastic about books and story telling. Twos can already be familiar with how books work, have their own favourites and choose to look at books themselves.
- Young children's request to have favourite stories 'again' is ideally suited for their learning. The repetition helps them to recall favourites and sometimes to tell themselves the story as they turn the pages. Twos can also show an awareness of narrative, telling or requesting their own stories (see the example on page 19).
- Children like a story read or told to pictures with plenty of expression in the words and your face. They enjoy dramatic pauses and repeating those phrases that they can say. Enthusiastic listeners to stories will have the motivation to want to learn to read, when they are ready. Reading is not just a technical skill; young children need to feel as if they are readers.
- Rich oral communication is a crucial basis for written language. Twos, threes and fours need plenty of relaxed experience of genuine conversation. They become confident with using language to explain, argue or recount. They get their thoughts out of their head through

Being a helpful adult

Two-year-olds will enjoy meaningful mark making. Give them time to explore this important step on the way towards emergent writing. They need:

- Generous amounts of stationery and ideally some that can be carried around indoors or outside – in a little box or carry-bag.
- Encouragement to use mark-making materials and, within a family home, clear boundaries around where and how it is fine to make marks and where it is not all right.
- Acceptance of what twos tell you they have done with their marks. If you use the word 'scribbling', then make sure that your tone communicates respect. Rising threes may soon say that they have 'written' something.
- To see you as a reader and a writer. If you know your spelling needs attention, then get it right. In the same way, let children see you as a counter and a measurer. Voice out loud what you are doing and link counting words and actions to why you need to count or measure.

Being a helpful adult

An important part of being a helpful practitioner to twos is sharing ideas and understanding with young children's parents. When you see the range of battery-driven toys and electronic systems marketed at families, it is hardly surprising when some parents quiz nurseries or childminders about when their two-year-old is going to know their letters and numbers.

Hold tight to your child development knowledge and do not be persuaded that partnership means you have to say, 'How soon would you like?' A better, more professional response would be: 'I'm so glad you care about early literacy – so do I/we. Please let me show you what I/we do.'

Settings or childminders who find ways to say and show, usually find that parents then say, 'Now I see what you mean'. If that leaves a few who still want their twos to do join-the-dot writing, then you, and your colleagues if you work in a team, need to be able to explain why this is not appropriate.

Use the same response if you encounter an inspector whose child development knowledge is shaky.

You can draw on useful websites and materials, such as the Literacy Trust, Basic Skills Agency and the Early Education leaflets (see Resources, page 53).

their mouth. Writing is not solely a technical skill. When they are ready, children need reasons to want to write and to feel competent about getting their thoughts in order.

- Nursery rhymes are enjoyable for young children and help communication, memory and the skills of hand movements. Familiarity with rhymes builds young children's understanding as it tunes them into the sounds and sound patterns that make up their language(s).

Young skills are hindered, not helped, by being pushed into handwriting exercises, flash cards or letter and number drills. It takes time for these symbols to have real meaning for children. Such early pressure can also undermine the necessary physical confidence. Large physical movements are just as important for the later skills of writing as finer coordinations.

- Large movements, such as playing with ribbons or large swirly movements with brushes, are important to hone the balance and skills that enable children to control pencils later.
- Trying to get two-year-olds to trace letters or other 'handwriting practice' displaces all the essential skills practice as well as convincing young children that writing is something boring that adults make you do.
- Many creative activities build the skills for writing (much later – when children are ready) . Very young children like to wield a paint brush, large crayon or chalk and make marks in whatever way they like. The practice builds the basis for the physical skills. But children are also building an intellectual understanding of mark making – 'When I make this movement, then I can create this swirl or that long line'.

For example

From the children in the Baby it's You project (Annette Karmiloff-Smith - see Resources, page 52):

- Her mother describes Polly, at two years three months who, 'likes scribbling, especially on important documents! Her spontaneous grip on the pencil is unorthodox but she accepts being shown a mature grip and maintains it'. One month later: 'We do drawing together: Polly draws a circle and then says triumphantly, "It's a cat!" She enjoys watching me write her name in large letters, naming the letters as they appear. (The naming is not consistent – she will sometimes call an O an egg!)' (page 128)
- Gillian's mother describes her daughter at two years ten months: 'Gilly just loves to use crayons and paints. She's very serious about her drawings, although usually they don't look much like anything to me. Sometimes it's a bit like a person – at least there's a round part with a line coming out of it. But she's very diligent and can literally stay with one drawing for an hour or so muttering to herself in a world of her own. She's more expansive with paint. We've tried finger painting which is dreadfully messy – I prefer her to do that at nursery school. But with a brush, if I hold onto the paint pot she actually does long lines quite artistically.' (page 130)

Building firm foundations

Sue Palmer and Ros Bayley describe seven strands to build strong foundations for literacy through the early years. They explain that their work 'has been developed in response to concern among early years practitioners that, in a multimedia world, children's language and listening skills are less well-honed than in the past. At the same time the "academic" demands of early education has increased – so, as oral language development has become ever more important, less and less time has been available for it' (*Foundations of Literacy* - see Resources, page 52).

Sue Palmer and Ros Bayley are talking about threes to fives in the English Foundation Stage. So their approach comes with increased emphasis when the focus is on two-year-olds. They show that the most crucial building block for firm foundations is 'Learning to listen', closely followed by 'Time to talk', 'Music, movement and memory' and 'Storytime!' The approach is consistent with the practical advice in this book, not least the importance of rich oral communication – we need to give generous time to relaxed talking with children.

Really early mathematical thinking

Written numbers, rather like letters, seem obvious to adults as a form of communication. But you have lived with these symbols for years. To twos they are just meaningless squiggles so you do not need to rush young children into recognising written numbers.

Annette Karmiloff-Smith (see Resources, page 52) describes how even babies seem to have a basic idea of number, long before they can count, because they notice 'same' or 'different'. Five-month-old Sarah, part of the Baby it's You project, seemed to have a sense of how many toys should re-appear in a hiding game. Her parent had dropped one of the toys by mistake in a hiding and re-appearing game. Only two toys re-appeared on Sarah's highchair and she looked puzzled.

When you listen to young children, you will realise that two-year-olds are already working within an understanding of many basic mathematical ideas.

For example

- Harry (described by Cath Arnold - see Resources, page 52) at two years four months is interested in exploring size and fit, putting his cars and trucks into two lunchboxes. Harry spends time packing and carrying. On one occasion Harry rejected a truck that was too big to fit, but persevered in trying to shut the lunchbox with cars ranged on each side of the box. His older sister, Georgia, suggested to him, 'Put them all in one side and it'll close'. Harry followed her suggestion and the box shut. At two years four months Harry was watching a Pingu video and said, 'one baby', 'two babies' and 'three babies' but he held up five fingers. He is getting the idea that he can represent quantity but has not cracked the one-to-one correspondence between fingers, counting and items. By two years six months Harry has not only the idea of number names but is able to use the words accurately for counting items and finger pointing for one item at a time. At two years ten months Harry counted 'five of us' correctly.
- Tanith at just two years imitated her older brother in asking us what specific written words said. At this age she confused written letters with numbers; she believed all the marks 'said something'. She liked to say, 'one, two, three, four', but without reference to anything in particular. At two years six months Tanith could finger point to count a small number of objects. She liked to count up to five and sometimes made it to ten. At just over three years, Tanith could reliably finger point to count actual objects, like books or bricks, up to five or six or more. She was confident counting up to ten, but liked some help with an adult voice joining in from ten to 20.
- At two years six months Ben has a clear concept of two and seems to identify confidently what looks as if it is one and one more. He accurately says that there are two trains and uses two correctly for other sets of two. He spontaneously uses words to describe a range of positional concepts, such as 'in', 'out', 'off', 'down' ('sit down') and 'under'. Ben uses words like 'big' and 'little' correctly. He also shows a good visual check on size. For instance, he looks at the pretend French bread and says, correctly, 'that's too big' to put in his pretend toaster. But he judges correctly that the pretend slice of bread will fit.

Being a helpful adult

Look at any written or numerical material in your setting, or in your home if you are a childminder.

- Is writing there for a good reason? Does it effectively say, 'Read me!'?
- What about single letters on friezes, bricks, fixed to plastic toys, on quilts – anywhere? Think about why the letters are there and what they say.
- If single letters do not say anything at all, why are they there? When children are genuinely interested in letters then they are better served by plastic or magnetic letters that can be moved around and held.

Do the same for numbers – think about what job they are doing, what they communicate to children.

- Single numbers may be there for a good reason, because they are the number on the front door or the parking bay for bikes.
- What about a number frieze? Do children look at it or is it now just wallpaper?
- A book with items to count may work better, or a story where a group of cats or other items become less and then re-emerge.
- Do children see you reading and writing numbers? Do they see and hear you counting – for a practical reason?

Food for thought

Susan Morton describes an action research project in a Fife nursery class. The team wished to improve their practice supporting children's understanding of number and other mathematical concepts. The children were aged from three to five years of age, but the practical conclusions can help to ground good practice for the twos.

The team made some progress by offering adult-planned number activities which the children enjoyed. But closer observations of child-initiated activities showed that a great deal of early maths was going on naturally through children's chosen play and conversation - counting out loud and using numbers in the writing area, exploration of spatial relationships and awareness of shape. However, little of this learning had been noticed by staff or recorded in the children's profiles. The three main conclusions of the project were that:

- 'Number and mathematical understanding improved when children's experiences' (the self-chosen ones) 'were used as opportunities to advance their knowledge and understanding.'
- 'Skills were improved with repeated opportunities to practise them, for example counting out at snack time, counting each other at homebase time, using positional vocabulary outdoors and in the gym.'
- 'When we showed children that we used numbers either in talking and/or in writing, they copied us.'

The full report is available on www.scre.ac.uk/spotlight/spotlight88.html

When you watch young children you will notice that they are exploring early mathematical ideas through their play. When you spend time alongside them, you can pick your moment to introduce the appropriate words.

For example

During the enjoyable mornings I spent watching Ben play, it was possible to see him using mathematical awareness around concepts that I did not hear him put into words.

- Ben was interested to build a single-brick wide tower. He added the plastic bricks one or more at a time. When the tower became wobbly from the height, he was content for me to hold it steady while he kept adding. I commented that it was such a tall tower. Soon the tower was too tall for Ben to reach to add more bricks, so he got a child-sized chair and continued to build. He seemed to understand what I was saying as I moved my hand to show 'nearly as tall as you/taller than you/even taller than you' standing on the chair.
- Ben worked confidently with his hands, for example fitting together the tracks of his train set (a simple round hole and shape lock). He fitted the train and trucks together and noticed straightaway if he did not have a hole and shape that would fit, turning the items around so that they would connect together. On this occasion, Ben did not voice his thoughts out loud but busily got on with building his track.
- Ben drew with his crayons, creating dots and lines in a deliberate way

The *Birth to Three Matters* component cards offer plenty of guidance for play opportunities that provide meaningful early numeracy. 'Making connections' suggests the flexible use of play materials, such as counting farm animals or sorting socks into pairs - a simple 'two of a kind' experience. 'Healthy choices' advises duplicating materials that are popular and good resources to help two-year-old turn taking. But basic number understanding is also supported when there is more than one wheeled trolley, three watering cans and maybe two copies of a favourite book. Tidying-up time in nursery is also finding time. The same opportunities present themselves in a family home. I recall getting my children to search for 'the last two pieces of our seaside jigsaw' or 'the three spoons missing from our tea set'.

Rising threes may know the order of low numbers, perhaps that three is always less than four. Like many abstract ideas, older twos and young threes benefit from a personal link. A given number is 'Mine. I'm three' or 'That's our number', as in their house or flat number. Rising threes and young threes can become alert to numbers all around them, like the letters in writing that they see indoors and on the street - what Cathy Nutbrown calls environmental print. There is also environmental number and you help two-year-olds by responding to their interest, as well as voicing out loud when you need to use numbers for making a purchase, preparing food or cooking and finding a route.

Genuine creativity in arts and crafts

Young children learn from sensory experiences and most of them really like to get their hands stuck into playdough, make buns or cakes or see what happens when they tip water into the outdoor digging area. Toddlers and two-year-olds like to wield a paintbrush – even a medium size grown-up paintbrush with a bucket of water outside. They learn mark-making skills and show two-year-old creativity with tools like large crayons, chunky chalks, their own hands and different kinds of materials and tools.

For example

- Look at the *Birth to Three Matters* video: the sequence in 'A competent learner' where young children are preparing what the narrator says are shopping lists. The children look as if they are having a good time, but observe how they hold the pens with a fist grip and one child moves the pen from one hand to her other. Twos and young threes like 'grown-up' stationery and they benefit from having pens and pencils along with the crayons, chunky chalks and larger paintbrushes. But this sequence is a good reminder why you should not be in a rush to give twos a 'proper' pen and expect them to do writing.
- Look at the *Birth to Three Matters* CD-Rom video excerpts: the same sequence is on each component for 'A competent learner'. Very young children are absorbed with glue and spreaders. These twos and toddlers are allowed to take their time. Some are keen to watch the glue drop. Some obviously enjoy the spreading action. All of them can explore choices from the resources of what, if anything, they put on the glued paper.
- Supportive practitioners let twos concentrate and explore. I have several distinct examples from nurseries where confident practitioners have watched toddlers and twos spend their entire time at a similar table spreading glue carefully on their own hands. It has been described to me how even young twos have waited patiently for the glue to dry and then focused eyes and fingers to peel off each section of glue at a time. Nothing tangible was made that afternoon but a great deal was done and learned.
- There are many useful sequences in the video that comes with the Foundation Stage information pack for parents. Look at the example of threes and fours getting their hands into paint – mixing, poking, doing hand prints when they wish and really finding out what happens when... Bear in mind that these children are three and four years old and the video was designed to support practitioners in explaining good Foundation Stage practice. There are no sequences about every child having to make the same starfish, because 'it's in our topic' or harassed to do something for the display board 'because otherwise

Being a helpful adult

The value of creative activities for toddlers is undermined when practitioners feel they have to make sure that there is a neat end product. The *Birth to Three Matters* pack is clear that good practice is to provide materials, be close to help if required but to give young creativity free rein, within the boundaries of safety.

The 'Being creative' component card recognises that this balance can feel like a challenge for some practitioners, 'For young children the process of creating is more important than an end product. Be sure that everyone understands the importance of the process so that they do not expect "products" from babies or very young children'.

The card goes on to comment, 'When children do produce a painting, your response and the way it is displayed are important.' Certainly, twos no longer regard a painting or collage as theirs if practitioners feel impelled to tidy it up, make it 'nicer' or cut around it to fit the current topic. I have listened to sensible, reflective practitioners who have been provoked to rethink their daily practice by twos who no longer recognise 'their painting' on the display board.

parents ask, "Hasn't he done anything today?"' So such unwise practice must be even less appropriate for the twos!

Anxious practitioners can be tempted to hold little hands to direct printing or sticking. I have even known unreflective practitioners take a painting or model away 'before she spoils it' and finish off work to make it look 'nice'. Practitioners sometimes justify the intervention, and insist that young children make something by saying, 'But parents expect it'. But, much as with sensible early literacy, good partnership is not to harass two-year-olds into 'creative conveyer belt' activity. Parents who understand their young children will realise how much has to be the work of the practitioners. Parents who really believe their two-year-old did all this careful cutting and sticking will develop wildly unrealistic expectations for the future!

Photographs, as well as conversation, are a much better way to show and share genuine two-year-old creative activities. This option then easily encompasses the fine tower of bricks or incredible 'deep, deep hole' which twos have created. Young children understand the idea of pictures and are thrilled to have a permanent record of something that matters to them. Nursery teams and childminders who use a camera all say that young children soon identify what of their own 'work' they want to have captured on film.

Creativity in thinking and pretend

Two-year-olds know enough of their world to play around with reality. They can use their imagination and creativity to tell simple stories and to weave pretend into their play, even if they do not yet show the lengthy role play of threes and fours. Creative development is only partly fuelled by arts and crafts, as enjoyable as appropriate activities can be for twos.

- Creativity is also shown by the flexible thinking that enables twos to try several different ways to get their wheeled trolley around a tight corner.
- A creative two-year-old, in a well resourced learning environment, is enabled to think 'outside the box', because nobody is saying, 'Where do you think you're going with those!' For instance, large cotton reels can be used for threading but also make a fine boundary fence for the animals.
- A good store of pine cones and corks can be any food that two-year-olds want for their pretend cooking. A large cardboard box can be absolutely anything and sometimes more than one thing at the same time.

For example

At two years six months, Ben's play reflects what he knows of real life and his own powers of imagination.

- Ben uses his language to start and continue all kinds of play. In his bedroom Ben began a game by explaining to me, 'I'm going to hide for you' and then 'I'm going to hide in there' (the wardrobe). Ben enjoyed the game, when I acted as if I did not really know where he was and was surprised when he appeared.
- Ben was busy with creative pretend play. He offered cups of tea to me and to his mother, remembering about milk and sugar. He set out a table for pretend tea with cups and saucers, plates and spoons in sets. He offered me some pretend bread. I said that I liked Marmite on my bread but not in my tea. Three times Ben joked and spooned pretend Marmite into my tea cup.

Food for thought

An activity does not genuinely support children's creative development just because paint or similar materials are on the table and the planned activity is labelled 'creative'. It is important to reflect on some or all of the following:

- Could children choose whether to take part in the activity – when, for how long or at all?
- Could they just watch if they preferred to be an observer?
- How much work had you done on the materials beforehand? Had you cut out shapes, chosen colours for them, offered a model to copy? Why?
- How much genuine choice did children have about how they used the available materials and tools?
- Have you had an activity lately that was not on a table, for instance boxes and tubing outside in the garden?
- Who decided when any piece of work was finished? The child or an adult?
- Who decided if there was an end product at all? If something emerged, how was it kept and where? Who decided if it was displayed and how?
- Could children return to the activity after they had wandered off? Was there somewhere to place work in progress? (Nurseries and childminders can have a shelf for safe storage of items, like woodworking, that can take children some time.)

- Ben has Baby Sam – a small doll with his own pushchair, blanket and baby cup. He was careful with Baby Sam and asked me to sit the doll on my lap when we were building with the Lego bricks.
- Ben's mum is expecting a baby. Ben was proud to show his new bedroom at the top of the house and explained that his old bedroom would be for the baby. He showed me the pram, explaining that it was 'for the baby – in Mummy's tummy'. Ben demonstrated how the cot mobile worked and re-arranged some baby items in the cupboard to his satisfaction. I asked Ben if the photos in his own bedroom are of him as a baby (they are) and he did not answer. I asked his mother, Louise, and she confirmed that Ben does not currently believe that he ever was a baby.

When twos are busy concentrating with materials of their choice, you can see them practise all the physical skills and hand-eye coordination that they will later use for handwriting – when they are ready. For instance:

- Ben spent 15-20 minutes working with playdough on his own kitchen table. He was interested in a simple machine that Louise had recently bought for him. A pressing mechanism squeezed playdough through one of a choice of shapes. Ben was intrigued to find out how the new machine worked and was willing to press hard to operate it, although it was easier for an adult to start the press.
- Ben liked making 'snakes' and used a range of plastic tools to work with the long shapes or other pieces of playdough. Ben used his language to explain and direct with, 'We have to make a snake first' and 'Shall we make another one?' He explained, 'I'm cutting it for you' and asked his mother, 'You put some eyes on' (the snake).
- Ben used his fingers, a knife, scissors and a pastry crimper. He looked carefully and lined up the tools to cut, poke holes and make a series of deliberate marks. He selected, held and used each tool with care and looked carefully to see what he had done, before continuing or selecting a different tool.

A healthy child

Food for thought
The introduction board for the 100 Languages Exhibition (that shows the work of the early years centres of Reggio Emilia, Northern Italy) includes a significant sentence: 'Children's timing and rhythms demand the utmost respect. They need adults to stand by them to counter the increasing pressure to make them grow up too fast'.

This message reminds us of the central importance of care and caring for the under twos. They will be damaged when adults force them to join an intellectual rat race.

Research into how young brains develop has shown how under threes have a strong disposition for learning. But they progress intellectually one step at a time, just as their ability grows to jump, climb and run.

Unfortunately, some commercial products try to persuade us that earlier must be better. What do you make of the image I once saw for one electronic system? A baby of about seven or eight months is sitting on an adult's lap looking at the flat pad. Speech bubbles are shown, saying 'five toothbrushes' and the even more bizarre 'five colours'! The words might as well say, 'Get this baby to climb to the top of the climbing frame'.

Physical and emotional well-being go together

Babies are designed to be social and we should worry when young children do not connect with adults. Two-year-olds will not feel emotionally secure if their important adults – practitioners or parents – are mean with their time and attention. Even good quality indoor and outdoor spaces and generous supplies of play resources will not replace what two-year-olds gain from kind, attentive adults.

- **The sixth principle in *Birth to Three Matters* is that, 'Caring adults count more than resources and equipment'.**
- **One of the key messages drawn by the Scottish research review was that, 'Practitioners are the most important resource in out-of-home provision for children less than three years old. Practitioners should be able to "tune in" to each infant or toddler as they share and learn, matching the child's communication pattern and interests and meeting the infant's crucial need for companionship'. (Research summary, page 7)**

For example

The Social Toddler by Helen and Clive Dorman provides picture stories of two children, both aged two years seven months, at a very early stage of settling into their nursery.

- Malachi (page 250) was happy on the first day and ran to join in the play activities on offer. But the next day he was not happy at all. His mother and nursery teacher, Ellen, gave him time and patience to express his feelings but Malachi continued to be distressed. Briefly, it looked as if Malachi might settle if he could have a particular toy car. Then another child drove it away and Malachi was distraught. After a while it was clear that Malachi wasn't going to be happy that day, so Ellen and his mum agreed that he would return home. There was no sense of criticism and Malachi would be welcomed when he tried again another day.
- Elizabeth (page 252) finds it difficult to leave Nicola, her mother, and clings to her. Her older brother Shane is happy to play. Ellen offers to take Elizabeth and carries her inside. She cuddles Elizabeth on her lap while they play together with some dough. Elizabeth is once more distressed when she sees her mother through the window. Nicola is having the opposite problem with Shane who wants to stay, but it is not one of his days at nursery. Elizabeth needs to be carried and cuddled by Ellen for some time and then they go outside. Only then is Elizabeth willing to be put down and she starts to play. She still wants Ellen to be close enough that they are in direct physical contact. Finally, Elizabeth lets go when she, Ellen and Peter, another child, blow some bubbles together. But at the end of the nursery session, Elizabeth runs straight up into her mother's arms.

Knowing where I am – the importance of routine

Young children like to be able to predict and anticipate some of their day. Of course, surprises are nice sometimes, but two-year-olds can be unsettled by a day or session that moves on or changes without obvious markers. Caring routines for twos are partly about their continued need for personal care, although they will be steadily sharing in their own care. Adults need also to value and show respect for the regular routines of the day or session.

For example

The Windham nursery school team have put a lot of thought into how to support children to manage the transition from one part of the daily routine to another. Bear in mind that these children were three or four years of age and I visited towards the end of the summer term. They still needed the caring support that is stressed for twos within this book.

Windham works within a well-resourced indoor and outdoor learning environment for the children. There is much careful adult planning, but it is discreet. The planning shows itself through resources, adult-initiated activities offered with choice and practitioners who are playful and conversational. The team have put thought and care into a clear routine at the end of each session.

- Children are eased, with warning, from self-chosen play towards tidying up, sometimes followed by physical games that adults lead in the outdoor area (traditional games like 'Oranges and Lemons').
- The routine moves towards sitting in one area of the room to have their fruit, with the helpers of the day being the only children on the move.
- Practitioners touch children gently on the head to move five or six at a time from the fruit circle to the informal rows for singing. There is then a short and active singing time as a group.
- All the practitioners are involved, so any individual children who find the transition more difficult to manage can be guided by an adult sitting close to them.
- The team use specific short songs to ease children from movement to listening. Part of the singing time is also using sound makers to shake and tap in a rhythm that includes a stop phase.
- A small number of songs include action. There is the opportunity for a few children each time to join two practitioners at the front of the group to do the appropriate actions with props.

The boys and girls in the example from Windham nursery school still needed the careful routine created by the team. Twos and young threes struggle to cope if group time in a setting is not eased with similar care. Young children benefit from routine that is predictable but not fierce. They really like to know what will happen within their day, whether they are in nursery, with their childminder or in their own

Being a helpful adult

Emotional security for young children is built on continuity between home and out-of-home care. You help through your friendly communication with parents and other family carers.

- Your early relationship-building with parents shows how you want to understand their child's personal preferences and care routines. You are not trying to take over and change established patterns.
- Share edited highlights of what children have done during the day. Twos may still struggle to find the words to explain, especially if a happy experience needs some new words. Make sure you give parents the chance to talk about what happens at home, and not just about problems.
- Some nurseries and childminders welcome tangible links with home: family photos that are given as much importance as those taken by practitioners, home items on display or part of interest tables, a personal treasure box for children who find it reassuring to handle simple items from home during their day or to look at photos.
- Reassure parents that they will be the continuity in their child's life. You are pleased to be part of the child's time now, but parents will be there when the child has moved on from your nursery or care as a childminder.

home. Then, even the twos can begin to anticipate what will happen next and start to organise themselves a little.

Young children, right up to and including the early years of school, need to feel at ease within their daily routine. When children are sure of routines, they feel confident to organise themselves more – a skill that children need as they enter their school years. In contrast, children are anxious when adults do not take time and trouble to manage their expectations and create predictability in the day. Children then spend precious emotional energy searching for clues about what happens next, wondering 'Is this what I'm supposed to be doing?' 'What do the adults want this time?'

Twos often face some disruption to the predictable pattern in their home life. Quite a few twos experience the significant changes that accompany the arrival of a new baby. Some go through disruption in family life caused by their parents separating. A good basis of partnership with the family will help you deal with how young children express their concerns.

For example

Harry was two years eight months when his parents told him and Georgia that they were going to separate. His father felt that it did not sink in for Harry until the family actually moved into two separate homes. However, as Cath Arnold describes (*Observing Harry*, page 60), during the period between being told and the move, the family diary showed that Harry was tearful and revealed anxieties through his play. Aged two years ten months, Harry was playing with Teddy Tom (a small teddy). The diary entry said, 'Harry carried Tom carefully, saying "He's got no daddy" then "He's got no mummy" – "no brothers, no sisters". At the same time, Teddy Tim (a larger teddy) is the "fixing man" for the cars'.

Of course, we have to be cautious about how to interpret what young children show through their play. But it does seem likely that Harry, like other young children of his age, was expressing his uncertainty through play, more than in directly spoken words to family members.

Doing it myself - sometimes!

It is important that young children develop competence in the wide range of skills that it is possible for them to learn within their first three years. But we also want babies, toddlers and very young children to grow in confidence. They need a sense of 'I can' or 'Maybe I could' and 'I'm going to have a go'.

Confidence needs to go hand in hand with competence. Otherwise, young children have skills that they choose not to use, perhaps because they feel what they manage is never quite good enough. Confidence in very young children is shown partly by persistence, as they keep trying to make a sand castle that does not collapse. Or they make every effort to tell you about the 'big, hairy cat on the high wall', although they are missing key words to describe this thrilling event.

For example

Ben at two years six months shows a 'can do' outlook through many aspects of his development.

- Ben has a substantial vocabulary and constructs sentences that include different types of words. His phrases are largely grammatically correct for what he wants to communicate.
- Ben uses his fine physical skills for drawing and, at the same time, he uses language skills to comment on his actions and plans: 'Oops! There's some paper in the way', 'I'm going to take this one off' (the paper round the crayons) and 'It's a bit noisy' (when he was doing fierce dot making with a crayon).
- Ben asks questions with confidence: 'What is happening?' 'What is (someone) doing?' 'Where are we going?' 'What's under there?' He expresses his own wants and wishes. He is also confident to share his knowledge. For instance, Ben showed me his toy fire engine and immediately made the link to real ones, saying 'They put out fires'.
- Ben understands everyday information and communication technology such as television and a remote control. He recognises audio tapes and knows how to use the controls of the music player in his playroom. Ben has generalised from familiar equipment and he recognised similar machines and equipment in my house. Ben was confident that he could work my remote control or that we could get the tapes to work.
- Ben understands that some of his toys need batteries and that they stop making the sounds if the batteries have run down. He also understands that he needs an adult to put the batteries into a toy.
- Ben moves around confidently – walking, running, climbing and managing up and down stairs – in his own home and elsewhere.
- Ben uses careful looking and fine physical skills as he works with materials for building and constructing. He looks equally carefully at his books, turning the pages and opening the flaps one at a time.

The tenth principle given in the introduction booklet to *Birth to Three Matters* is that, 'Young children are vulnerable. They learn to be independent by having someone they can depend upon'. Two-year-olds can already have learned many abilities and want to use them. If twos are to be able to take over and practise their own self-care skills, you need to:

- Make the time so that young children can practise their dressing and undressing, hand washing and toileting, mealtimes and all the other routines and skills that are best learned within the earliest years.
- Value that these abilities matter and admire what is involved: fine physical skills, sequencing, concentration and a motivation to keep trying.
- Show genuine pleasure at what twos can do.
- Resist the temptation to hurry them or re-do a self-care task or domestic routine to your own, adult standards.
- Use all the opportunities that naturally present themselves. You do not have to design and plan activities to support this area of learning.

So, the regular routines of personal care are not something to hurry through to move on to other activities that are defined as important early learning. Two-year-olds who feel relaxed, who have not been rushed through their personal care routines, will be ready to enjoy play resources in your setting. Given time and adult patience, young children will share in their own care and contribute to looking after their nursery or home environment. This long drawn-out process is a directly valuable source of learning: for physical skills, communication, simple forward planning and understanding a sequence.

Food for thought

Practitioners or parents who feel 'it's quicker if I do it' need to ask themselves what kind of children we all want to raise for the next grown-up generation.

- Children who feel competent, yet able to ask for help if needed?
- Children who feel they will rarely meet tough adult standards?
- Or children who are convinced they have people who will dress them and mop up after them, as if they were a highly paid celebrity?

Practitioners who undervalue care in favour of a restricted vision of early education need to answer the question, 'So, when are very young children going to learn crucial skills of self-reliance?' The best time to learn a skill is when you can see you need it and are keen to learn.

Certainly, there is full support for time and respect for care in the English *Birth to Three Matters*. There are many examples of giving children personalised care and choices within their care routine. The video shows a high value for care with a long sequence of a practitioner taking time over changing a young child and helping him with his own hygiene.

The Scottish *Birth to Three* leads with responsive care and respect shown through care.

The birth to three materials are supported by other good practice guidance such as the *Key Times* video and pack (see Resources, page 53). Important messages include:

- Allowing time within the day or session for children to be able to deal with their own dressing and undressing – whether for outdoor clothes or to have a nap.
- Twos like to be part of putting out the sleep mats or bedding in full day nurseries. I have seen young children fully capable of joining in this task, and proud to be trusted. Some twos and young threes are also aware that their peers like to have their bedding or mat in the same place, with a cuddly, or other personal items ready to greet them at sleep or rest time.
- Within drink, snack or mealtimes, cutlery and tableware can all be chosen so that children can help with this routine. Small jugs help children to do their own pouring. An easily accessible cloth lets them wipe up any spillage.
- The timing of toileting and hand washing should enable children to be as independent as they wish. Adult help is always on offer but not imposed.
- The *Key Times* file, 'Growing mobility, dexterity and independence', gives the wise advice that, 'Going to the bathroom is recognised as an interesting activity for babies and toddlers so plenty of time is allowed for this and opportunities for independence are maximised.' (page 5)
- The end of the same *Key Times* file section has a positive focus on

'Organising routine times as prime times of the day'. The resource lists as prime times – arrival and separation times, home time, washing, toileting and changing times, mealtimes, sleeping or rest times.

A positive approach to routines is also linked with a proper key person system (see page 9).

Twos appreciate the calm when you give time and plan routines like mealtime, so that everything is close. It will distract children if you bob up and down on a regular basis. In a family home and any group setting you should equip the routine so children can do a lot themselves. Supportive adults also keep to the familiar routine and the layout of the learning environment. You do not change corners or the contents of a resource box, except for a good reason. Then you let children know what will change, with a simple explanation of why. You also discuss with them any changeovers of pictures or photos that are on display; they then feel a sense of ownership.

For example

In the *Key Times* file, 'Their curiosity and desire to explore the world around them' you will find the useful example of two-year-old Tim.

- The practitioner had noticed that Tim had recently become interested in trying to dress himself. In conversation, Tim's father said that at the weekend Tim had two tantrums because he wanted to put on his shoes and socks. Tim could not manage it but refused to accept any help. Tim's key person then made some flexible plans to help Tim. Wellington boots and waterproofs were kept by the garden door, so that all children could get dressed to go into the garden. Children who could put on their boots were encouraged to help the children who were still struggling. The practitioner had also made sure there was a good supply of shoes and hats in the dressing-up area. It would be more straightforward for Tim to 'do it myself' in that part of the routine.
- Tim's key person decided that the sleep time routine was the best opportunity to help Tim directly. So she took time to let Tim undress himself. She pulled his sock to his heel, so he could manage the rest and let Tim put his clothes away in his own basket, before settling to sleep.

This example shows how partnership with parents blends with a flexible approach to planning for individual children within the out-of-home care situation.

A second example of supportive personal care is described in *Key Times* within 'The interest in developing social relationships with their peers' (page 4).

- Amin, aged two, was crying because he wanted to go on the library trip barefoot. Adam, the practitioner, explained, 'I know you like going barefoot but the stones outside will hurt your feet. You can stay here and play with your shoes off or put them on and come with us. Which do you want to do?' Amin insisted, 'Go with no shoes'. Adam replied, 'Sorry, that's not a choice. I tell you what. You can wear your own nice trainers or you can wear these nice red nursery wellies. You choose and put them on while we go and put our names in the outing book but we can only wait five minutes for you'. Amin put on the Wellington boots and joined the group.

This good example highlights how supportive and kind adults can behave. It would not have been responsible to offer the choice of going barefoot, but Amin did not have to cope with a no-win situation. He benefited from practical support from a practitioner who offered choices within a boundary, and was patient. Amin was given the time to consider and made his choice.

The best nurseries have a home-like feel and that is why examples from children's home life are equally relevant to guide good practice in group settings. One of the many picture stories from *The Social Toddler* (Helen and Clive Dorman) shows choice for young children within a home setting.

- Ethan, who is two years three months, is keen to choose his own clothes for the day. His mother, Julie, creates a manageable choice by laying out two possible choices of each item and Ethan is able to make his choice one item at a time. Julie then tucks the other clothes out of sight and helps Ethan to get dressed (page 244).

Food for thought

Young children flourish when they hear your thanks in words and a smile. Twos (or threes and fours) do not need to be 'paid' with stickers or treats and it is unwise to establish this expectation with young children. Simple appreciation works as the best form of encouragement.

You can sometimes use a meaningful activity incentive with twos, for example, 'That was such a speedy tidy-up job. Well done! That means we have time for an extra story'.

Two-year-olds do not really understand the symbolic nature of stickers, or similar forms of reward, although they will not turn them down. However, children will soon ask, 'Will I get a sticker?' when you request them to take on a routine task. Perhaps you answer, 'No – we all help out here'. Then young children may legitimately decline to accept that task. They are not being 'uncooperative' or any other negative behaviour label. Children are responding to the situation set up by the adults. Their reaction shows they understand that you have established a token economy in your nursery or home.

If you face this situation, it is well worth reflecting how you offer encouragement and show appreciation. If parents have started to track how many stickers their child receives, then definitely do some serious rethinking.

Examples from the Baby it's You project (see Resources, page 52) show a respect for the complexity of the self-care skills and the patience needed from adults – in these examples from a parent:

- Gillian is two years nine months and her parent explains: 'Gilly's preferred activity these days is dressing herself. She spends hours getting the buttons done up and usually sadly she's got the button in the wrong button hole so she has to keep starting again. But she simply won't let me help her. We've often gone out with her coat unevenly buttoned, but she's happy!' (page 113)
- When Jimmy is just two, his parent describes the situation: 'Tooth brushing is a really serious moment. He stares at himself in the mirror and often the paste drops off his brush when he's not looking. So I have to help him start again. He squeezes the tube but I hold on to it just in case. He's getting quite good at moving the brush along his teeth – I've shown him the up-and-down method, but he seems to prefer the to-and-fro method' (page 128).

Once young children feel competent in some aspects of their own care, they feel a real pleasure at helping younger or less competent children.

- At just two years of age, my son Drew used to choose his baby sister's first daytime outfit of clothes each morning. We kept Tanith's clothes in the bottom shelf of a cupboard that Drew could easily reach. He soon learned to pick a vest, an all-in-one baby gro and a cardigan. We always accepted the combination he chose, even if in our eye the colours clashed. Once Tanith was changed and dressed, Drew would usually take the baby brush and gently stroke her hair.

Helping in domestic routines

Sensible planning allows you time to respect two-year-olds' need for personal care and to value their wish to be active helpers in regular routines. Young children learn through being an active helper. Ordinary, domestic events support children's learning in a holistic way. The *Birth to Three Matters* component cards, and the video, are clear that it is inappropriate to keep young learning in separate compartments.

- Young children experience personal satisfaction from being a helper to adults and other children. They feel trusted and like the sense of 'that's my job' or 'me and Amy did that'. A friendly atmosphere establishes that 'we all help out in our nursery' (or a child's home-from-home with a childminder).
- When two-year-olds are active in a tidying-up routine, they learn about same and different, what fits and what does not and putting resources back into the right basket or box.
- Young children sometimes learn about working together with another child as a partner, because 'we need two of us – this basket is heavy' or 'I'm doing the plates and Gavin is doing the cups.'
- Children's involvement in the routines for snacks, drinks or mealtimes provides a meaningful context to use numbers for counting. Laying the table requires physical skills alongside visual coordination, as does serving a friend with another helping of vegetables.
- Young children often chat when they are part of a shared domestic activity, like sorting out the fruit. They use communication skills in a relaxed, one-to-one context with an adult or perhaps one other child.

For example

Look at the video excerpt in the *Birth to Three Matters* CD-Rom under each component of this aspect.

- You will see and hear young children involved in the regular nursery routine of preparing food for their guinea pigs. The children are actively involved in sorting out and cutting up the food. They are not just watching an adult do this. The practitioner is sitting with the children. She has organised for enough time and she comments in an encouraging way on what the children do.
- The atmosphere is friendly and relaxed. For instance, a boy starts to eat a cracker and the practitioner asks if it tastes nice rather than telling him not to eat it. She then asks what it tastes like and confirms that it is called a cracker.

- As the routine continues, the practitioner comments in a meaningful way to name items and what the children are doing. She voices out loud what she is doing, for instance taking the roof off the guinea pigs' house.
- The children are fully involved in the whole routine from preparing the food, to going out to the garden and giving the animals their food. They then watch and discuss whether the guinea pigs like crackers or not.

In the *Birth to Three Matters* video there are several sequences within 'A Healthy Child' that clearly value mealtimes. In 'A Strong Child' there is a sequence that shows a two-year-old dealing with the consequences of a spillage.

- A young boy has spilled some sand and, without being prompted, gets a dustpan and brush and tidies it up. The voiceover describes him as 'surprisingly competent'. I disagree with 'surprisingly', as do practitioners who enable two-year-olds to be active helpers within a nursery or family home. Many twos are well able, and keen, to carry out this kind of task. All adults need to do is make the tools available, give children time to learn and be appreciative of their efforts.

A picture story in *The Social Toddler* (Helen and Clive Dorman) shows how children like to be involved in ordinary domestic routines.

- Ethan at two years three months wants to take items one at a time out of the washing basket. He takes a bath towel and, using his legs to provide a surface, adeptly rolls the towel by working it down the length of his legs. He then repeats the rolling process with other items and hands them to his mother. From the picture story it is uncertain whether Ethan's actions are directly helpful to his mother, Julie, or not. But she thanks him and has the rolled-up items on the work surface (page 262).
- Ethan is in his own home but it is equally important to create opportunities in non-home settings for children to take part in such domestic routines. You may not let children go into the utility room in a nursery, but it is perfectly safe to involve children in washing dolls' clothes. I have known nurseries who engage the twos in folding up the clean, dry washing. Young children have been enthusiastic about folding, sorting into pairs, and they enjoy a chat at the same time.

Learning on the move

The *Birth to Three Matters* support materials for all the aspects show that use of physical skills is definitely not the poor relation in terms of child development. There are many visual examples (photographs and video) and written advice on the cards that demonstrate that children learn by being on the move and using all their skills. Physical development is a named area in every early years curriculum document of the four nations that comprise the UK. Young children need to have plenty of time and space to use their physical skills. Their development is put at risk when practitioners define concentration as staying still and, even with some twos, as 'doing your work' before children are allowed 'free play'. The materials related to 'A Healthy Child' give a very clear message that young children need to be able to explore indoors and outside, with choice and the resource of a kind and playful adult.

For example

Look at the *Birth to Three Matters* video. There are plenty of examples throughout about the importance of being able to move, as well as stay still when children choose.

- The section related to 'A Healthy Child' shows that good practice, even for these very young children, is to enable two-year-old adventures and physical exploration. Look at the children practising their balance on the snake and the chain, and their clambering wall. The twos are able to learn about concentration through physical skills, relaxed practice and how to judge risk within a safe enough environment.
- Compare this footage with what you can see in the Foundation Stage video designed for use with parents. The clear message related to these slightly older children is that they are still doing so much learning through moving about and a great deal outdoors, not just inside.

I enjoyed watching a mixed group of twos, threes and fours in St Mark's Nursery School.

- They relished having buckets of water and paintbrushes in the garden on a warm summer's day. The children were given a free choice about how to use the materials.
- The younger children were fascinated by simple brushing onto the paved surface. They seemed to be interested in how the water disappeared in the heat of the day.
- The slightly older children experimented with the chalks that were also available. Some of them chose to chalk around the water then watched as the wet area retreated and shrunk. Their chalked outline was a clear indication of how far the wet area had dried out – good early science!
- The flexibility of materials in the outdoor area meant that the two-year-olds, the youngest in this setting, were able to access sturdy climbing equipment, the caterpillar tunnel and wheeled vehicles as they wished. Since they could make easy choices, there was no need to have equipment especially for them.
- The painting easel and water tray were outside. During the afternoon, two young girls organised their own outdoor book area under a large sunshade. They were able to lay out cloths and bring out books in a manageable container, because all these materials were available.

At Windham Parent and Toddler Drop-in, young children can move freely between indoors and the outside area.

- Jamie and Sara were joined by Maria in a large wooden rocker. The children could not make the rocker work without help. So an adult kept up the momentum with one foot discreetly on the back of the rocker.
- Sara experimented with 'look no hands' by lifting her hands off the holding rail and putting them directly up. She managed to keep her sitting balance and looked pleased with her achievement. She then repeated the feat.
- All the children were able to keep up a conversation with the adult at the same time as rocking and keeping their balance. They showed their ability to concentrate on more than one task at the same time.
- I was close and I could hear what the children said. But, unlike the practitioner, who was familiar with the children, there was a fair proportion that I could not understand. This is a timely reminder that there will always be a tuning-in period for an unfamiliar adult to understand most of what twos want to say.

The facilities and organisation of a nursery day should provide all the kinds of opportunities that two-year-olds can access in a home situation – their own family or the home of their childminder. Good practice in a group setting would be to enable any of these home examples to happen – perhaps in a slightly different way, but opportunities should be provided.

For example

A picture story in *The Social Toddler* (Helen and Clive Dorman) shows the delights of physical movement.

- Ethan at two years three months can bend at the knees to launch himself into the air. He likes to throw his arms and legs forward to move and land like a frog. He finishes in the same squatting position and shows his mother, Julie, that he can be a frog when he chooses.
- Later, Ethan shows his physical skills by climbing up the bookshelf to reach a video. He is capable but Julie has to get him down for safety. She follows her 'No' with the explanation that it is dangerous to climb up the bookshelf. Ethan can ask for any video he wants. This example is a useful reminder that, especially in a family home, two-year-old physical skills are used with a limited intellectual grasp of risk (page 238-9).

Harry's development is described by Cath Arnold, his grandmother (*Observing Harry: Child Development and Learning 0-5* - see Resources, page 52) .

- At one year 11 months Harry tried to copy his older sister, Georgia, who could do a headstand. 'He leaned forward resting his head and both hands on the floor without raising his feet off the floor. When Georgia did a headstand by putting her hands on the couch, he fetched a small chair, placed it next to the couch, then stood on it and threw himself forward onto the couch.' (page 44). Harry had done his best to replicate Georgia's actions to make a headstand, but he was too young too understand how the starting position becomes a fluid movement.

Over the year of being two, Harry spent a lot of time practising and honing his physical skills.

- At two years one month he could cut out one-handed, holding the paper in his other hand.
- At two years three months Harry became interested in a pump action container of cream. He took several tries before he worked out that one hand needed to be at the ready to catch the cream and the other hand then worked the pump action. The challenge seemed to be partly the physical coordination, but also fathoming out how this piece of domestic equipment worked. (Young children are often fascinated by pump action containers, such as liquid soap.)
- At two years three months Harry tried eating at a family barbecue from a long plastic salad spoon. He enjoyed using a pair of tongs to carry a sausage from a serving dish to his plate.
- At two years four months Harry got the small hoover and began hoovering the carpet. He got Teddy Tim and put his paw on the handle of the hoover and then did the same with Teddy Tom (Harry's little and large bears).
- At two years 11 months Harry had his first go at trying to hit a ball with a golf club. This proved to be a tough task. However, he enjoyed leaning the club against a post or a chair.

What should concern you?

There is great variation between young children and much will happen although in different patterns, over the year that they are two. Early years practitioners need to keep a firm grip on sound child development knowledge. You need to share this knowledge with parents and other family carers, as well as detailed examples of their child's learning while in your care.

Make sure that you do not become concerned about skills that are unrealistic for this age group. For example, young twos should not be expected to know a wide array of abstract concepts, especially if their important adults are trying to push these ideas through inappropriate methods and toys. On the other hand, two-year-old language development would usually have moved into spontaneous use of some descriptive words. Twos, whose expressive language includes naming and action words but no descriptive words at all, could be delayed in their communication and thinking.

Two-year-olds do not show 'poor' concentration because they are unimpressed by group story time or required to sit still and be quiet for long periods. On the other hand, you should notice a child who finds it hard to settle to any activity, whether a self-chosen experience or a friendly welcome to join an activity with an adult. Without leaping to any conclusions, you can make informal observations and talk with a child's parent. The pattern of a child's attention, or apparent inattention, might make you wonder about hearing loss.

It is possible to keep a watching brief and continue to communicate with parents. For instance, some 18-month-olds are already chatty, although most likely not easily understood by unfamiliar adults. Other toddlers of the same age have a limited number of words that they use, although parents will be reassured if their toddler genuinely understands much more in context. The slower starters often then take off like an express train to catch up their more chatty peers by around the second birthday.

However, attentive adults should expect spontaneous speech from the just twos. It is appropriate to be concerned if the weeks, and especially the months, roll by and an older two-year-old is not making utterances that you, as a familiar adult, can understand. Obviously, it is a different situation when young children show the fluency of a two-year-old in a language that you do not speak. Then you need to gain an idea, most likely from their family, how children are managing in their home language(s).

Emotional control and social skills are definitely work in progress for two-year-olds. They have a limited ability to wait and will run out of friendly options swiftly within a confrontation with another child. Twos need kindly adult support and a wise use of adult strength to make sure that they do not hurt themselves or others. You can help a great deal by holding realistic expectations about turn taking for twos in a group environment. You also need to make sure there are plenty of flexible resources that make give-and-take an easier option.

All twos welcome support over routines and transitions but you might notice young children who struggle more than their peers, even with all your help. Two-year-olds make the move into rich pretend play and making social contact with other children. Some twos will always be slower to warm up to friendships. But you should notice young children who have had time to settle, and still appear perplexed by play and social interaction that their peers take in their stride.

Two-year-olds, especially young twos, are still fine tuning their skills of movement, balance and making their senses of vision and hearing support their physical skills. Some twos will already seem more at home in their own body than their less physically confident peers. All children need plenty of practice with large physical movement as well as fine co-ordinations. Encourage the less enthusiastic climbers and jumpers with a manageable one bit at a time. You will then see if there is more to their reluctance than lack of experience combined with low confidence.
Some two-year-olds will join you and their family already has a clear understanding, possibly a diagnosis, of how a disability is affecting their child's pattern of development. Usual good practice for partnership applies: you talk with parents to understand their child as an individual with familiar routines, likes and dislikes. Parents will be able to tell you, as a childminder or the child's key person in nursery, about their child's current ability level and any special help that will be needed.

You would be expected to make reasonable adjustments to include children with disabilities or continuing health conditions that affect their development or behaviour. The legislation on disability discrimination does not insist that all children must be admitted, come what may. But it would be regarded as obstructive if early years practitioners refused a child for reasons like 'children must be toilet trained' or 'if children need medication then they should be at home'.
You are not expected to know everything about every disability. Good practice is to know how to find out more. The *Birth to Three Matters* cards have some practical ideas within the 'Meeting diverse needs' and illustrative advice through the case study sections to each card. You can build up a useful resource file from inserts available with magazines like *Practical Pre-School* and *Practical Professional Child Care.* There are some useful references in the resources list that follows.

Further reading and resources

- Arnold, Cath *Observing Harry: Child Development and Learning 0-5* (Open University Press 2003)
- Basic Skills Agency *Read and Write Together, Count and Figure it out Together* (1996) and *Read with me* (2004) (BSA Tel: 0870 600 2400 or look at the website www.basic-skills.co.uk)
- Bilton, Helen *Playing Outside: Activities, Ideas and Inspiration for the Early Years* (David Fulton 2004)
- Brennan, Carmel *The Power of Play: a Play Curriculum in Action* (Irish Pre-school Playgroups Association 2004)
- Bruce, Tina *Cultivating Creativity in Babies, Toddlers and Young Children* (Hodder and Stoughton 2004)
- Caddell, Dorothy *Numeracy Counts* (Scottish Consultative Council on the Curriculum 1998; available from Learning and Teaching Scotland)
- Campbell, Robin *Literacy from Home to School: Reading with Alice* (Trentham Books 1999)
- Clark, Alison and Moss, Peter *Spaces to Play: More Listening to Young Children* (National Children's Bureau 2005)
- Community Playthings *Spaces: Room Layout for Early Childhood Education*; also *Creating Places for Birth to Three: Room Layout and Equipment* (free, Tel: 0800 387 457 www.CommunityPlaythings.co.uk)
- David, Tricia et al *Birth to Three Matters: a Framework to Support Children in their Earliest Years* (2002 – research review that can be printed off the CD-Rom. Prolog will send a free summary research brief or you can buy the full report as a bound booklet Tel: 0845 6022 260)
- Dockrell, Julie; Stuart, Morag and King, Diane *Talking Time: Supporting Effective Practice in Pre-school Provision* www.literacytrust.org.uk/talkto yourbaby/talkingtimeproject.pdf
- Dorman, Helen and Dorman, Clive *The Social Toddler: Promoting Positive Behaviour* (2002 The Children's Project Tel: 020 8546 8750 www.childrensproject.co.uk)
- Edgington, Margaret *The Great Outdoors: Developing Children's Learning through Outdoor Provision* (Early Education 2002)
- Edwards, Anna Gillespie *Relationships and Learning: Caring for Children from Birth to Three* (National Children's Bureau 2002)
- Elfer, Peter; Goldschmied, Elinor and Selleck, Dorothy *Key Persons in the Nursery: Building Relationships for Quality Provision* (David Fulton 2003)
- Evans, Betsy *You Can't Come to my Birthday Party: Conflict Resolution with Young Children* (High/Scope Educational Research Foundation 2002)
- Featherstone, Sally and Beswick, Clare *Little Baby Book* series (Featherstone Education 2003 and 2004)
- Gladwin Mark *Consulting Children about Play* (Children's Play Information Service 2004 www.ncb.org/library/cpis)
- Healy, Jane *Your Child's Growing Mind* (Broadway 2004)
- Hughes, Anne and Ellis, Sue *Writing it Right? Children Writing 3-8* (Scottish Consultative Council on the Curriculum 1998)
- Karmiloff-Smith, Annette *Baby it's You: a Unique Insight into the First Three Years of the Developing Baby* (Ebury Press 1994)
- Kinney, Linda and McCabe, Jerry *Children as Partners: a Guide to Consulting with Very Young Children* (Stirling Council 2000 Tel: 01786 471177)
- Lewisham Early Years Advice and Resource Network *A Place to Learn: Developing a Stimulating Environment* (LEARN 2002 Tel: 020 8695 9806)
- Lindon, Jennie *Too Safe for Their Own Good? Helping Children Learn about Risk and Life Skills* (National Children's Bureau 1999)
- Lindon, Jennie *Helping Babies and Toddlers Learn: A Guide to Good Practice with Under Threes* (National Children's Bureau 2000)
- Lindon, Jennie *Understanding Children's Play* (Nelson Thornes 2001)
- Lindon, Jennie *Child Protection* (Hodder and Stoughton 2003)
- Lindon, Jennie *Understanding Child Development: Linking Theory and Practice* (Hodder Arnold 2005)
- Palmer, Sue and Bayley, Ros *Foundations of Literacy: A Balanced Approach to Language, Listening and Literacy Skills in the Early Years* (Network Educational Press 2004)

- Rich, Diane *More than Words: Children Developing Communication, Language and Literacy* (Early Education 2002)
- Scottish Executive *Birth to Three: Supporting our Youngest Children* (Learning and Teaching Scotland 2005, buy from LTS Tel: 0141 337 5000 or download from www.ltscotland.org.uk/earlyyears/Birthtothree.asp)
- Skinner, Carole *More than Numbers: Children Developing Mathematical Thinking* (Early Education 2001)
- South Lanarkshire Council *Learning for Living: An Early Years Curriculum 0-5* (1999 Tel: 01698 454470)
- Trevarthen, Colwyn et al *Meeting the Needs of Children from Birth to Three* (2003) on www.scotland.gov.uk/Topics/Research Go into Education and Training. To find the summary type 'Insight 6' into the search facility. To reach the full report use search for 'Colwyn Trevarthen'.
- *Special Educational Needs in Practice* (Step Forward Publishing 2002)

Websites

- Early Childhood Development – informative about the approach in New Zealand, four issues of an online resource about infants and toddlers, *The Importance of Brain Development* and three issues about *Creating an Empowering Inside Learning Environment* www.ecdu.govt.nz/running/whiria
- Early Childhood Unit *Listening as a Way of Life* - free leaflets Tel: 020 7843 6064 or download from www.earlychildhood.org.uk
- Early Education *Learning Together* series of free leaflets Tel: 020 7539 5400 or download from www.early-education.org.uk
- EPPE: The Effective Provision of Pre-School Education project www.ioe.ac.uk/schools/ecpe/eppe
- Learning and Teaching Scotland has a valuable early years section with materials to download: www.ltscotland.org.uk/earlyyears
- Learning Wales for information about the Foundation Phase and any future developments, also a parents section: www.learning.wales.gov.uk
- Literacy Trust has user-friendly materials and includes a link to the useful Talk to your Baby website: www.literacytrust.org.uk
- Parent Centre – a website developed off the main DfES site has useful material including a 0-3 section: www.parentcentre.gov.uk
- REPEY project Researching Effective Pedagogy in Early Years: Brief No 356: www.dfes.gov.uk/research/data/uploadfiles/RB356.doc
- Sure Start website has a range of downloadable information including three resource guides on *Working with Young Children from Minority Ethnic Groups, Working with Parents of Children Under Three* and *Working with Young Children who have Special Needs or Disabilities*: www.surestart.gov.uk/ensuringquality/birthtothreematters/trainingonbto3/resourceguides
- Zero to Three website www.zerotothree.org Wide range of information to download including the Brain Wonders section.

Video materials

- Channel 4 *Baby it's You* (Woodside Promotions 1994 Tel: 01372 805000)
- High/Scope UK *The High/Scope Approach for Under Threes* (1999) and *It's Mine! Responding to Problems and Conflicts* (2003) (Tel: 020 8676 0220)
- Manning-Morton, Julia and Thorp, Maggie *Key Times: A Framework for Developing High Quality Provision for Children Under Three Years Old* Video and resource binder developed by Camden Early Years. The materials are being reproduced by Open University Press (due out in 2006).
- National Children's Bureau *Tuning in to Children* Video and book (1997 Tel: 020 7843 6000)
- Sightlines Initiative Rising Sun Woodland Pre-school Project Video and booklets (2001 Tel: 0191 261 7666 www.sightlines-initiative.com)
- Sheffield University REAL Project *Early Literacy Education with Parents: a Framework for Practice* (1996 Tel: 0114 222 0400)
- Sure Start/DfES *Birth to Three Matters: A Framework to Support Children in their Earliest Years* Video, booklet, poster, cards, CD-Rom (2002, free from Prolog, DfES publications centre Tel: 0845 6022 260).
- Sure Start Foundation Stage Video and leaflets for sharing with parents. (2003, also from Prolog)

Acknowledgements

I have learned a great deal by running training days and leading conferences on good practice with under-threes and when twos are the youngest in a group setting. A heartfelt thank-you for the opportunity to listen and talk with a considerable number of early years practitioners, local advisers and development workers.

I appreciate the insights gained from visits to a wide range of early years settings and contacts with childminding networks. In connection with this book, I am especially grateful for the welcome offered by the staff and children at these settings and to parents for agreeing to my visit:

- Windham - a Partnership for Children (South London): thanks to Rosie Leonard (headteacher), Cherry Baker (deputy head) and Katie Erskine (responsible for the parent toddler groups at Windham) and their teams.
- St Mark's Square Nursery School (North London): thanks to Sheema Parsons (head), who has developed a consciousness based nursery education for two to sixes, and her team.

I would also like to thank the following individuals whose ideas on early years practice have been so valuable:

- Peter Elfer (senior lecturer, University of Surrey at Roehampton),
- The development team at Community Playthings, especially Martin Huleatt, Helen Huleatt and Martin Rimes.
- Lena Engel, head of the under-threes advisory team at the London Borough of Hounslow.
- All the members of the early years advisory teams of the London boroughs of Hounslow, Richmond and the LEARN team at Lewisham.

I have changed the names of any children from examples observed in settings. Otherwise I have retained the names used in any books or packs from which I have quoted. Drew and Tanith are my own (now adult) son and daughter and they have given permission for me to quote from the informal diaries I kept of their first five years. Thanks to Louise and Ben who made me feel welcome to join them so I could learn about Ben's two-year-old skills. Thanks to Louise and Kevin Browne who gave permission to use the examples of their son.